SCHOLASTIC

THE ULTIMATE BOOK OF
PHONICS WORD LISTS
FOR GRADES K–1

Word, Phrase, and Sentence Lists, Plus Games for Reading, Writing, and Word Study

LAURIE J. COUSSEAU AND RHONDA GRAFF

DEDICATION

To Joann Crawford, my mentor who taught me everything
I know about linguistic structure and who transformed
the lives of so many children and educators
— L. C.

To my truly remarkable mother, with love and
deep gratitude
— R. G.

Thank you to our editor, Maria Chang,
for her support and guidance.

SVP & Publisher: Tara Welty
Editor: Maria L. Chang
Creative director: Tannaz Fassihi
Cover design: Cynthia Ng
Interior design: Maria Lilja
Images © Shutterstock.com and The Noun Project.

ISBN: 978-1-5461-1383-6

CONTENTS

INTRODUCTION

"Teaching reading is rocket science."
–Louisa Moats, Ed.D.

To teach children how to read requires a deep understanding of language and linguistics. Our brains are hardwired to speak and listen, but not to read or spell.

As teachers, reading specialists, literacy consultants, and Orton-Gillingham trainers, we have used various programs and methodologies that teach reading. We recognized the need for resources to help teachers teach foundational skills in reading and writing. We wanted to create an easy-to-use, comprehensive resource that supports structured literacy instruction based on the science of reading.

The Ultimate Book of Phonics Word Lists for Grades K–1 contains lists of words, phrases, and sentences that feature the phonetic patterns and spelling generalizations children need to learn how to read. We've also included descriptions and explanations of various phonetic patterns to support decoding and encoding instruction.

This resource can be used in a variety of settings—across the three tiers of instruction, in general education and special education programs, and for homeschooled children. It should be noted, however, that this is a resource, not a curriculum.

How to Use the Lists, Games, and Assessments

The lists in *The Ultimate Book of Phonics Word Lists for Grades K–1* are organized by phonetic patterns/skills and build from words to phrases to sentences. We chose words, phrases, and sentences that are high utility and support the development of children's vocabulary.

Although the skills covered in this book are generally taught in the primary grades, many students struggle with reading and spelling acquisition well beyond first grade. For that reason, we've expanded this resource. While most of the words in the lists are basic-level words, you'll notice some of the words are in **boldface**. These words contain the same phonetic patterns but are slightly more advanced and can be used with older students who still need basic instruction. It is important to acknowledge that some students need basic reading instruction long past the early elementary years. We recognized that need and created a flexible, teacher/parent-friendly resource. A teacher, specialist, or tutor can identify the words that will best serve a child, group of students, or class.

DECODING ENGLISH

There are 26 letters in the English alphabet. These vowels and consonants come together in varying orders and combinations to form words. Children need to recognize these letters or combinations of letters in isolation and practice reading and spelling them in many words. There are 44 *phonemes* (the smallest unit of sound) that are represented by *graphemes* (letters or clusters of letters), and 72 *phonograms* (letters or series of letters that represent sounds or syllables). Some letters or combinations of letters have multiple pronunciations for reading, and some sounds have multiple spelling choices. For example, *ch* has three sounds to be retrieved for reading words: *chat, school,* and *chef.* The /k/ sound is represented by four spelling choices: *c, k, -ck,* and *ch.* Knowing when to use these sounds for decoding and for encoding is key to reading success. Children develop a discerning eye and ear. They become linguists themselves with this kind of deep word study.

WORD LISTS FOR READING

Choose the number of words for children to read based on each child's ability. Be careful not to overload them.

You can present the words to children by writing them in columns, a grid, or on cards that can be stored for future use. Children can read up and down a column or across rows in a grid. If children's first pass at reading the words is not automatic, have them read the words again to help improve fluency. You may need to model the proper pronunciation or assist with supporting strategies for decoding.

Whether using lists or cards, note how children are reading the words: correctly or correctly with automaticity. Also, take note of student errors, so you can provide guided correction and plan accordingly. In a future lesson, revisit those words for children to reread. Continue to provide other words with a similar phonetic pattern for further practice until the child no longer needs the review.

As an option, consider displaying the words in a pocket chart. After children have read through the words, ask questions or use prompts to enhance vocabulary. For example:

- *What word means . . . ?*
- *What word is the opposite of . . . ?*
- *Find a synonym for . . .*
- *Use a word in a sentence.*
- *Use two words in the same sentence.*

For a cumulative review, include words from previously taught patterns to create a mixed list. Additionally, plug the words into the game board templates to supplement single-word reading.

WORD LISTS FOR SPELLING

To build children's spelling skills, dictate words with the same phonetic pattern used in your reading lists. Include review words and words that children had trouble reading.

The number of words you dictate for spelling will depend on the child and may be fewer than the words provided for reading. Choose spelling words that are different from the words children have read but still follow the same pattern or skill. Create a master list of reading and spelling words so you can record errors for an individual child or a small group.

When you dictate a word for children to spell, it may be helpful to have them repeat or whisper the word prior to writing it to engage the auditory track. This helps enhance learning.

Collect children's spelling lists and use an error analysis diagnostically. For instance, a child who spells *bed* as *bid, red* as *rid,* or *bit* as *bet* is confusing short *e* and short *i* and needs more practice. By looking at the errors children make, you can note areas of confusion and plan instruction accordingly.

Invite children to read back the spelling words as another pass at fluency. Use the game board "Word! Wham! Wow!" (page 142) for spelling practice and reinforcement.

When children learn the phonetic patterns and generalizations, they no longer need to study words for a weekly spelling test. They can apply their knowledge and spell many words correctly without prior studying because of the depth of their understanding.

PHRASES AND SENTENCES FOR READING

Following each word list is a phrase and sentence list for each phonetic pattern. Use these to promote oral reading fluency and to help children see how to use the words in context. The sentences can be "scooped" for phrasing.

Encourage children to read the sentences several times with increasing prosody. Feel free to modify or extend the sentences based on children's needs. You can expand the sentences orally so children are not limited by spelling. For example, you may wish to expand the sentence, "The pans and pots banged and clanged," to "The pans and pots banged and clanged when we put them back on the shelf."

PHRASES AND SENTENCES FOR DICTATION

You can also dictate the phrases and sentences. Begin with a phrase or two, then dictate sentences in increasing length. Have children repeat the phrase or sentence prior to writing it on paper.

If children struggle to remember the sentence, have them repeat it a few times prior to writing it. Encourage them to cluster phrases and clauses and to visualize the sentence.

Teach children the importance of rereading their work to check for accuracy by using the acronym CHOPS. Have children reread the sentence they wrote and check off each letter to see whether their sentence is accurate. Does it have capital letters where needed? Is it neatly written? Does it include all the words in the correct order? Is it correctly punctuated? Is every word correctly spelled? (A teacher may need to check the spelling.) This is a great way to reinforce important aspects of writing sentences.

> C – capitalization
> H – handwriting
> O – order of words
> P – punctuation
> S – spelling

Afterwards, have children read back their sentences for more practice with fluency.

VOCABULARY

An enriched vocabulary can improve understanding. The Simple View of Reading formula shows that reading comprehension is the product of strong decoding and strong language comprehension (Gough & Tunmer, 1986; Hoover & Gough, 1990).

Use the word lists to create vocabulary cards that can be used for review. You can find a template online. (See page 8 for more information on how to access the supplemental online resources.) Revisiting the words on multiple occasions in various ways helps children incorporate the words into their vocabularies.

Explore words in depth with children, helping them understand how to use the words in sentences. Note synonyms and antonyms. There are many opportunities for vocabulary exploration using the word, phrase, and sentence lists as a springboard.

GAMES

Included in this resource are 10 reproducible word games and activities that provide fun ways to reinforce the phonetic patterns and skills. Customize the blank game boards to highlight any pattern or skill. Since all the games and activities require children to read words, we recommend that an adult be present to check for accuracy.

Use guided questioning to help children understand why they made a mistake and to help them fix it. Encourage children to explain the strategies, rules, and patterns they are using. For example, *Why is that vowel short? Why would you use* -tch *instead of* -ch? Children develop a deeper understanding when they can explain why.

Make extra copies of each game to send home for practice and reinforcement.

ASSESSMENTS

Online, you will find informal progress-monitoring assessments for most of the skill levels in the book. Assessments for word reading, phrase reading, sentence reading, and spelling are included.

We also provide teacher record sheets to support good recordkeeping and anecdotal note-taking. Each teacher record sheet has space allocated for two different assessments— a pre- and post-test.

We have also included blank assessments and blank teacher record sheets along with detailed instructions for teachers and parents to customize their own assessments.

SUPPLEMENTAL ONLINE MATERIALS

In addition to the assessments, we also provide lists of function words, content words, and irregular words, and other useful resources online. To access these materials, go to **www.scholastic.com/phonicswordlists** and enter the password **SC766601**.

We hope you enjoy using this resource as much as we enjoyed creating it!

The Ultimate Book of Phonics Word Lists for Grades K–1 © by Laurie J. Caruana and Pamela Craff Scholastic Inc.

Glossary of Phonetic Terms

TERM	DEFINITION	EXAMPLE
Affix	A morpheme that can be added to the beginning or end of a word—a prefix or suffix	**re**visit**ed**
Breve	A symbol used to code a short-vowel sound	˘
Closed Syllable	A syllable with a single vowel closed in by a consonant or consonants; the vowel sound is short.	map, mask hen, help pin, pick cot, cloth rub, rush
Consonant	A speech sound partially blocked by teeth, lips, and/or tongue; these are classified as voiced, unvoiced, continuant, or stopped.	*b, c, d, f, g, h, j, k, l, m, n, p, q, r, s, t, v, w, x, z*
Consonant Blend Cluster	Two or more consecutive consonants that maintain their individual sounds but are coarticulated	**sk**ip **fr**og **cl**am be**nd**
Consonant Digraph	Two consonants that have one sound; these often contain the letter *h*.	*ch, sh, th, wh, ph*
Content Words	Words that have a clear semantic meaning in a sentence	The **red fox ran quickly**.
Continuant Sound	A consonant sound that can be held	"mmmmmmmmm" "sssssssssssssssssssss"
Controlled Words	Words that a child can decode based on a specific continuum of skills already taught	If a child just learned short vowels and closed syllables, a sentence with controlled words should only include words with skills taught to date and not words with long vowels or more advanced syllable types.
Decodable Words	Words that can be sounded out and contain predictable phonetic patterns	e.g., V-*e* *fame, time, home, theme, fume*
Decoding	Sounding out a word and blending to say the whole word	
Encoding	Spelling and the ability to write a word based upon the speech sounds	Spoken word: s/k/oo/l Written word: *school*
Function Word	A word whose meaning is based upon the grammatical or structural relationship with the other words in a sentence	Often linking verbs She **is** a dancer.
Grapheme	A letter or letter combination that represents a single phoneme; could be two or more letters	*sh*, as in *wish* *igh*, as in *night*
Irregular Word	A word that is not decodable because it contains uncommon sound-symbol correspondences and is not spelled the way it sounds	s**ai**d

TERM	DEFINITION	EXAMPLE
Long Vowel	A vowel that says its name; long *u* says /ū/ and /o͞o/.	bake, stay me, wheel lime, sky hole, toast few, mule
Macron	A symbol used to code a long-vowel sound	¯
Morphemes	The smallest unit of meaning that includes prefixes, roots, and suffixes	in vis ible
Multisyllabic Words	Words that contain more than one syllable	fan/tas/tic (3 vowels = 3 syllables)
Open Syllable	A syllable that ends with a single vowel, which has a long sound	he hi no flu pa/per mo/ment
Orthographic Mapping	The mental process of forming letter-sound connections to secure the spellings, pronunciations, and meanings resulting in automatic sight recognition of a word	
Phoneme	Smallest unit of sound in spoken language; there are 44 phonemes represented by 72 written phonograms.	w/ay 2 phonemes ch/e/ck 3 phonemes
Prefix	A morpheme that comes before a base word or root that modifies its meaning	**re**turn **pre**dict **un**happy
Schwa	Although there isn't a specific letter to represent schwa, it is a vowel that often sounds like a short *u* or short *i*; it is found in an unstressed syllable; the symbol for schwa is ə.	**a**way pil**o**t jack**e**t
Scope and Sequence	A logical ordering of phonetic skills and spelling generalizations	
Short Vowel	A vowel sound that is not obstructed in a closed syllable	sit jump spend
Sight Word	A word that is recognized immediately; these may be regular or irregular.	said (irregular) say (temporarily irregular)
Stop Sound	A consonant sound that is stopped by the airstream and cannot be held	/b/, /p/, /d/, /t/
Syllable	A word or part of a word with a spoken vowel sound	
Syllable Types	There are reliably six syllable types where the pattern denotes the vowel sound.	closed (*not*) open (*no*) V-e (*note*) r-controlled (*star*) vowel team (*rain*) C-*le* (*maple*)
Suffix	A morpheme attached to the end of a base or root word that modifies the meaning or grammatical function	wind**s** wind**ed** wind**y**
Unvoiced	A consonant sound produced without vibration in the throat	/k/, /f/, /h/, /p/, /s/, /t/
Voiced	A consonant sound produced with vibration in the throat	/b/, /d/, /g/, /j/, /l/, /m/, /n/, /r/, /v/, /w/, /z/

The Ultimate Book of Phonics Word Lists for Grades K-1 © by Lavinia Coureau and Rhonda Graff, Scholastic Inc.

Short a

The first vowel sound children typically learn is the short-*a* sound. When making the /ă/ sound, the lips are not rounded and the front of the tongue is low in the mouth. Children find it helpful to have a key word that helps guide the articulation, such as *aaaapple*. Draw out the vowel sound to emphasize it.

Short-*a* Words

-ab			
cab	**lab**	**blab**	grab
gab	**nab**	crab	scab
jab	tab	**drab**	**slab**
-ad			
bad	had	pad	**tad**
dad	lad	**rad**	glad
fad	mad	sad	**shad**
-ag			
bag	**sag**	**zag**	flag
lag	tag	brag	**snag**
rag	wag	drag	**stag**
-am			
bam	ham	Sam	**cram**
cam	jam	yam	**sham**
dam	**ram**	clam	swam
-an			
can	man	tan	Fran
Dan	pan	van	plan
fan	ran	**bran**	**span**

-ap

cap	nap	**yap**	snap
gap	**rap**	**chap**	strap
lap	**sap**	clap	trap
map	tap	**flap**	

-at

bat	hat	rat	flat
cat	mat	sat	**spat**
fat	pat	chat	that

-ax

ax	**lax**	**sax**	wax
fax	Max	**tax**	**flax**

-ack

back	**rack**	**clack**	**slack**
hack	sack	crack	snack
Jack	**tack**	**flack**	stack
lack	Zack	quack	track
pack	black	**shack**	

-act

act	**fact**	**pact**	**tract**

-amp

camp	lamp	champ	stamp
damp	**ramp**	**cramp**	**tramp**

-and

and	hand	sand	stand
band	land	grand	**strand**

The Ultimate Book of Phonics Word Lists for Grade K–1 © by Laurie L. Cousseau and Rhonda Graff Scholastic Inc.

-ant			
pant	**rant**	**grant**	plant

-ash			
cash	**sash**	flash	splash
mash	crash	smash	trash

-ast			
cast	last	past	blast
fast	**mast**	**vast**	

-ath			
bath	math	path	

More /ă/ Words			
gasp	raft	ranch	**clasp**
mask	**task**	branch	**grasp**

Short-*a* Phrases

cat nap	tap tap tap	trash on the path
on a mat	jam on the bag	glad to do math
cat on a mat	gap in the mat	grab bag
sat on a mat	tap and rap	flat tan hat
nap on a mat	sat in the bath	mad crab
hat on a rat	can chat with a rat	damp rag
sat on a bat	can pack a bag	grand plan
rad cap	can pack a snack	hand clap
ran a lap	gab and chat	crab on the sand
gas in the van	black and tan	sand on the ramp
sap on a rag	crack in the bat	swam at camp

Short-*a* Sentences

The lad is glad.	Sam has a plan.
Wag the flag.	Grab the bag.
Pat the sad cat.	Sam will pack a bag.
The rat sat on a hat.	Dan has a van.
The cat had a nap.	Can a yak have a bath?
Dad sat in the tan van.	I had a chat with a yak.
The tag is on the bag.	Grab a bran snack.
Sal had sap on the rag.	Clap your hands fast.
Val put gas in the van.	Dad and Brad had a chat.
Rap with a rat and a ram.	Snag a flat cap.
Don't jab a yak.	That cat jams in a band.
The bat had a crack.	The crab swam to the raft.
Fran will pack a snack.	The clam sat on the sand.
The sad lad sat in the van.	Sand is on the black mat.
Dan swam with Dad.	Fran has a map of the path.

The Ultimate Book of Phonics Word Lists for Grades K–1 © by Laurie J. Cousseau and Rhonda Graff, Scholastic Inc.

Short *e*

The /ĕ/ sound may the hardest of the short vowels to articulate. The front part of the tongue is mid-height in the mouth. The lips are not rounded. Use the key word *eeeeedge* to guide the articulation. For a visual cue, run your finger along the edge of your hand.

Short-*e* Words

-ed			
bed	red	**bled**	**shed**
fed	Ted	**bred**	sled
led	**wed**	**fled**	**sped**
-eg			
beg	leg	Meg	peg
-em			
gem	**hem**	stem	them
-en			
Ben	men	**yen**	then
den	pen	**zen**	when
hen	ten	Gwen	
-ep			
pep	**rep**	**prep**	step
-et			
bet	let	pet	wet
get	met	set	yet
jet	net	vet	**fret**
-eck			
deck	**peck**	speck	**wreck**
neck	check		

-ell			
bell	**jell**	yell	smell
cell	sell	**dwell**	spell
dell	tell	shell	**swell**
fell	well		

-elt			
belt	melt	**dwelt**	**knelt**
felt	**pelt**		

-ench			
bench	**drench**	**stench**	**wrench**
clench	French	**trench**	

-end			
bend	lend	**tend**	spend
end	**mend**	blend	**trend**
fend	send		

-ent			
bent	lent	tent	went
cent	rent	**vent**	spent
dent	sent		

-ept			
kept	**crept**	slept	swept
wept			

The Ultimate Book of Phonics Word Lists for Grades K–1 © by Laurie J. Cousseau and Rhonda Graff Scholastic Inc.

-ess			
Bess	**bless**	guess	stress
less	**chess**	press	**tress**
mess	dress		

-est			
best	pest	**vest**	chest
jest	rest	**west**	**crest**
nest	test	**zest**	**quest**

More /ĕ/ Words			
elk	help	next	**cleft**
elm	left	**self**	shelf

Short-e Phrases

ten red hens	in the wet pen	pep and zest
hen in a pen	Meg the red hen	slept in a bed
red hen in a den	can check the bell	a red sled
fed ten red hens	can tell Ben	the best nest
a wet net	a wet shell	the best tent
will get a pet	a red dress	ten bent pegs
the vet's pet	less mess	in a red tent
met a vet	the jet sped	mend the pen
fed ten men	peg on the deck	test on chess
a wet jet	can get the net	bell in the dell
a red bed	next to the den	felt the shell

Short-*e* Sentences

Ted is in the shed.	Ned fed ten hens.
Meg will get a bed.	Ben slept in a tent.
The net got wet.	Rest in the nest.
Fred had ten hens in a pen.	The step on the deck is wet.
Get ten red hens in the pen.	The hen had the best nest.
Ben kept his pet in a pen.	I left my pen in the den.
Meg fell off the bed.	Don't step on the chest.
Em will get a pet.	Ren swept up the mess.
Ted got his pet to the vet.	Let's mend the wet net.
The vet's pet is a red hen.	Press the red dress.
Ed fed ten red hens.	Help me mend the dress.
Gwen fed ten men.	That red hen is a pest.
The jet is in the red shed.	Ed lent me his chess set.
The jet sped west.	You have a speck on your neck.
Don't beg for a sled.	Clem has pep and zest.
The hens slept in a bed.	The elk went west.

Short *i*

To articulate the short-*i* sound /ĭ/, raise the front part of the tongue high in the mouth. The lips are not rounded. A visual cue and key word can be *iiiiiiitch*.

Short-*i* Words

-ib			
bib	**jib**	crib	**glib**
fib	rib		

-id			
bid	kid	**grid**	slid
did	lid	**skid**	**squid**
hid	rid		

-ig			
big	**gig**	pig	**wig**
dig	**jig**	rig	twig
fig			

-im			
dim	**rim**	**grim**	**slim**
him	Tim	**prim**	swim
Jim	**brim**	**skim**	trim

-in			
bin	pin	chin	skin
din	tin	grin	spin
kin	win	**shin**	twin

-ip			
dip	tip	clip	ship
hip	**yip**	drip	skip
pip	zip	flip	snip
rip	**blip**	**grip**	trip
sip	chip		

-it			
bit	kit	sit	**flit**
fit	lit	**wit**	quit
it	pit		

-ix		
fix	mix	six

-ick			
Dick	Rick	chick	**slick**
kick	sick	click	stick
lick	**tick**	**flick**	thick
Nick	**wick**	quick	trick
pick	brick		

-iff			
cliff	sniff	stiff	**whiff**

-ift			
gift	**rift**	**drift**	**swift**
lift	**sift**	**shift**	**thrift**

-ill			
ill	hill	**till**	skill
bill	kill	will	spill
dill	**mill**	chill	still
fill	pill	drill	thrill
gill	**sill**	grill	
-inch			
inch	pinch	**clinch**	**flinch**
finch	**winch**		
-ing			
bing	sing	**cling**	sting
ding	wing	**fling**	string
king	**zing**	sling	swing
ping	**bling**	spring	thing
ring	bring		
-ink			
link	rink	blink	**slink**
mink	sink	drink	stink
pink	wink	shrink	think
-ish			
dish	fish	wish	swish
More /ĭ/ Words			
disk	milk	**quiz**	with
hint	mint	**silk**	chimp
list	quilt	wind	this

Short-*i* Phrases

pig in a wig	a pink wig	drip on his chin
a big rip	a big pink pig	did a quick trick
will pin the rip	six pink wigs	trick with a stick
a big fig	pins in the tin	stick pin
bit the big fig	dip in the chip	six big sticks
will zip and yip	kids on the hill	a chill wind
in a big pit	dig on the hill	the pink dish
did a jig	the big ship	a big twig
a jig with a pig	a big chimp	hid in the quilt
lid on the bin	fish on a dish	will skip and flip
in the big bin	fish fins	will flit and flip

Short-*i* Sentences

Pick up six sticks.	Pick a big fig.
Sid bit a big fig.	The kid had a big grin.
Dip the chip in the dish.	Get a grip on the twig.
Spit out the big pit.	The kids on the hill will zip.
The pig had a pink wig.	I wish for a trip on a big ship.
A pig in a wig can sit on the hill.	Tim can do a quick trick.
Will did a jig with a pig.	Dip and spin in the wind.
Dig up the big stick.	Don't slip and trip on the hill.
Put the pits in the big bin.	She had six pins in the tin.
Jill did a jig on the hill.	Stick this list in the bin.
Will you click on the link?	Can a fish swim in a dish?

Short o

The short-o sound /ŏ/ is made with a round mouth, like the letter o. Circle your mouth to provide children with a visual cue. Another fun way to introduce this sound is to have children sing oooooopera.

Short-o Words

-ob			
Bob	lob	sob	knob
cob	mob	blob	slob
job	rob	glob	snob
-od			
cod	pod	clod	shod
mod	rod	prod	trod
nod	sod		
-og			
bog	fog	log	slog
cog	hog	clog	smog
dog	jog	frog	
-op			
bop	pop	drop	prop
cop	top	flop	shop
hop	chop	glop	slop
lop	clop	plop	stop
mop	crop		

-ot			
cot	lot	tot	**plot**
dot	not	**blot**	**slot**
got	pot	**clot**	spot
hot	rot	knot	**trot**
jot			

-ox			
box	**lox**	ox	**pox**
fox			

-ock			
dock	sock	clock	knock
lock	**tock**	**crock**	shock
mock	block	**flock**	**stock**
rock	**chock**		

-ond			
bond	fond	pond	blond

-oss			
boss	**moss**	cross	**gloss**
loss	Ross	floss	

-oth			
moth	cloth	**sloth**	

More /ŏ/ Words			
mom	lost	soft	stomp
on	**romp**	**prom**	

Short-*o* Phrases

a hot dog	top of the box	a lost moth
got hot	hop hop hop	a lost sloth
hot pot	on top of the dog	socks with dots
a dog and a frog	fox in a box	a lost sock
a hog and a dog	job for an ox	pot of stock
dog on a jog	ox on top	moss on a rock
frog on a log	ox on the dock	lost in the fog
jog in the bog	will chop the log	will cross the pond
frog in the bog	tick tock	a flock on the pond
will bop and hop	on the clock	not a slob
will pop the top	will stop the clock	fond of frogs

Short-*o* Sentences

The frog can hop on a log.	The hog is not a slob.
Stop that dog and hog!	The frog got on top of the dog.
The fox got in a box.	The frogs hop on the dock.
Pop the top on the box.	The clock went tick tock.
Tom put the top on the box.	I'm not fond of cod.
The top of the box went pop.	Don't drop the log.
Get the hot pot on top.	Don't trip on the rock.
The hog and dog got lost.	The crock pot is so hot.
That's a job for an ox.	I lost my socks with dots.
Hop, hop, hop on top.	Dot got spots on her top.
Hop on the rock at the pond.	A glob of slop got on my top.

Short *u*

To make the short-*u* sound /ŭ/, the corners of the mouth rise up as if you are smiling. Use "thumbs up" as a visual cue with the key word *uuuuuup*.

Short-*u* Words

-ub			
cub	rub	club	**shrub**
dub	**sub**	**grub**	**snub**
pub	tub	scrub	stub
-ud			
bud	**dud**	**spud**	thud
cud	mud		
-ug			
bug	**lug**	tug	shrug
dug	mug	chug	slug
hug	pug	plug	snug
jug	rug		
-um			
bum	**mum**	drum	strum
gum	sum	**glum**	swum
hum	chum	plum	
-un			
bun	**pun**	sun	**stun**
fun	run	spun	
-up			
cup	pup	**sup**	yup

-ut			
but	**gut**	**jut**	**rut**
cut	hut	nut	shut

-uck			
buck	**puck**	cluck	snuck
duck	**suck**	**pluck**	stuck
luck	tuck	**shuck**	truck
muck	yuck		

-uff			
buff	puff	fluff	**scuff**
cuff	ruff	**gruff**	stuff
huff	**bluff**		

-ull			
cull	gull	**lull**	**null**
dull	**hull**	**mull**	skull

-umb			
dumb	**numb**	crumb	thumb

-ump			
bump	jump	**frump**	**slump**
dump	lump	grump	**stump**
hump	pump	plump	thump

-unch			
bunch	lunch	punch	crunch
hunch	munch	brunch	scrunch

-ung			
hung	sung	**flung**	stung
lung	**clung**	sprung	swung
rung			

-unk			
bunk	junk	**flunk**	**spunk**
dunk	sunk	shrunk	stunk
hunk	chunk	skunk	trunk

-unt			
bunt	**punt**	**blunt**	**stunt**
hunt	**runt**	grunt	

-ush			
hush	rush	crush	**plush**
lush	blush	flush	slush
mush	brush		

-ust			
bust	**gust**	must	**crust**
dust	just	rust	**trust**

More /ŭ/ Words			
bus	**fund**	much	plus
buzz	Gus	such	

Short-*u* Phrases

tub of mud	will tug on the rug	my bud the pug
bug in a mug	fun to hug a pug	gum on the drum
bug in the cup	a glum pug	hunt for bugs
rub a dub dub	will tug on a jug	just a gust
dug in the mud	dug up the bugs	dust and rust
fun in the sun	cubs in the tub	lump on a stump
run in the sun	slug in the tub	a bump and a lump
pug on the rug	snug bug in a rug	a bump on a rump
bug in a rug	duck in the muck	spun a drum

Short-*u* Sentences

Hug a bug on the rug.	I must dust the drum.
"Yup," said the pup.	My bud is a pug.
Hum with a chum.	The cup has dust in it.
We had fun in the sun.	The cubs hunt for nuts.
Lug a big jug.	The bugs are snug in the rug.
My mum can tap on a drum.	The pug and the bug are chums.
A bug swum in my mug.	Yuck, there is a slug in the tub.
We dug in the mud for slugs.	The stump has bugs on it.
There is mud on the rug.	A duck does not cluck.
That plum was mush.	The truck is stuck in the muck.
The pug sat on the rug.	The pup dug under the shrub.

Flex Between Short Vowels

When children first learn vowel sounds, flex between two sounds to help them distinguish between the different sounds. Use the assessment record sheets (online) to identify any vowel-sound confusion. Start with this list and then generate more word pairs.

Word Pairs

ban/bin	fog/fig	pat/pit
Ben/bun	fox/fix	peg/pug
Bob/bib	hip/hop	pen/pin
cub/cob	hut/hot	pop/pep
cut/cot	leg/lug	pot/pet
dot/den	nap/nip	rap/rip
fat/fit	nut/not	sap/sip

Mixed Short Vowels Phrases

a big pet	a lot of gum	a nut to crack
bit a plum	dug a pit	hid in the shed
tap or tip	on the dish	thick fog
Sam's red cap	can sip from a mug	jot on his pad
a wet mop	jog and run	zig and zag
in the red tub	on his hip	cut on a leg
can hop up	lots of jam	mad at him
rag on a rug	a fun job	cub in the den
sat on the cot	hid it in a red bag	in the cab
on the big map	a pen cap	not in luck
will step on the log	does not quit	thick or thin
on the bus	jam with a bun	moth wing

Mixed Short Vowels Sentences

Jim has a job.	Nat has a test.
The cat licks the pan.	Shut the box.
Put the cup on the big mat.	Set the chips next to the dip mix.
Jan will jog with the pup.	Put the peg in the tin can.
Tim can jot on his pad.	The dog got in the tub.
The pot has a lid.	Pat the pup and the cat.
Dad can get gas for the van.	Ed will nap on the soft cot.
Jen has a cup of nuts.	Liz can sit in the sun.
Did the duck get fed?	Tom led the pup to the tub.
Fred has a bump on his leg.	Rick went for a jog.
Peg got gas for the van.	I had jam with a bun.
Zeb will zig and zag.	Can you tip or tap on the drum?
Sip the drink in the mug.	Get in the cab.
Sam fell and got a cut on his leg.	It is hard to see in the thick fog.
We sat on the cot to rest.	Gus has a cut on his left hip.
Step on the log, but do not fall.	The red hen is in the tub.

/k/ Spelled c

The /k/ sound can be represented by the letter c or k. Children often have difficulty choosing which letter to use when spelling. We use the letter c before the vowels a, o, and u, as in cab, cat, and cut.

/k/ Spelled c Words

ca			
cab	cast	cake	car
can	cash	came	card
cap	catch	cape	cart
cat	call	case	**carp**
camp	cage	cave	care
co			
cob	cone	cord	count
cod	coal	cork	court
cog	coat	corn	cow
cot	cold	coin	come
cost	comb	couch	could
cu			
cub	cut	cute	curl
cud	cube	curb	curve
cup	**cure**	**curd**	

/k/ **Spelled** *c* Phrases

cap on a cat	a cute cape	cards at camp
a cup on a cot	can of corn	can care for the cat
can call a cab	can catch the carp	corn on the cob
cod or clams	can cut the cake	cart of coal
cute cow	cubs in the cave	cow in the cave
car on the curb	camp in the car	can count the cows
cold cup	came in a car	coat on the couch
a cape or a coat	cup of curds	can count the cash

/k/ **Spelled** *c* Sentences

Call the cute cat.	Could you call a cab?
Mom cut the cake.	They came in a car.
The cup was cold.	Cam combs her curls.
Let's camp in the car.	Carl sat on the curb.
The cap did not fit the cat.	We can play cards at camp.
She has a cute cape.	Put your coat on the couch.
The cap and the cape look cute.	Can I nap on the couch?
I had corn on the cob.	The cat curls up on the cot.
The coals are in the cart.	How many coins are in the cup?
The cows pull the cart.	Count the cubs in the cave.
Eat the corn on the cob.	The cute cat came home.
Can you catch a carp?	Can you count the cows?

/k/ Spelled *k*

Because the /k/ sound can be represented by the letter *c* or *k*, children often have difficulty knowing which letter to use when spelling. Tell them we often use the letter *k* before the vowels *i* and *e*. Explain that the letter *k* is less common than *c* as a choice.

/k/ Spelled *k* Words

ki			
kid	kit	king	kind
Kim	kick	kite	kitten
kin	kiss		
ke (/k/ initial position)			
kelp	**keel**	keep	key
kept			
ke (/k/ final position)			
bake	like	wake	spike
bike	make	Blake	spoke
cake	poke	quake	stake
hike	**sake**	shake	strike
lake	take	snake	trike
ke (/k/ before y)			
donkey	monkey	turkey	

/k/ Spelled **k** Phrases

a big kid	will bake a cake	kelp in the lake
in the kit	can make a kite	like to hike
kite kit	bike or hike	will kiss Kim
keep the key	bike to the lake	will wake the snake
kind king	will take the cake	monkey and donkey
kept the kite	snake in the lake	a kind kitten

/k/ Spelled **k** Sentences

The kid kept the kite.	The kids like the kind king.
The kite came in a kit.	Let's hike up to the lake.
Let's bake a cake.	We can bike to the lake.
We saw a snake at the lake.	I like the lake at dusk.
The kind kitten takes a nap.	Bake a cake for the king.
Kim gives her dad a kiss.	The kids like to hike.
Let's bake a cake for the kids.	Shall we bike or hike to the lake?
Two kids kept the key next to the rock.	The monkey and donkey like to take naps.

Mixed c and k

The /k/ sound can be represented by the letter c or k. Children often have difficulty knowing which spelling to use. We use the letter c before the vowels a, o, and u. We often use the letter k before the vowels i and e. The letter k is less common than c as a spelling choice.

Mixed c and k Phrases

kind cat	snake in the cave	key to the car
will kick the can	will catch the kite	can kiss a cow
cute kitten	can kick hard	can keep the comb
the cat's kittens	king's cape	can keep the cup
kept in a cage	will call the king	will catch the donkey

Mixed c and k Sentences

Kim has a cute cat.	The cat's kittens were so cute.
Keep the kind cat.	The king came in a cab.
Kick the can on the curb.	The kids tried to catch the kite.
What color is the king's cape?	The kittens were cold.
The kids at camp catch cod.	Don't cut the kite's cord.
Can the king kick a ball?	Take the kite to camp.
The cute kitten keeps napping.	Mike kept the cans in the closet.

/k/ Spelled *ck* (final position)

The /k/ sound at the end of a one-syllable word following a short vowel is often spelled -*ck*; for example, *sack* or *pick*. Once children learn -*ck*, they then have three choices to spell the /k/ sound: *c*, *k*, or *ck*. Knowing the three spelling choices for /k/ and understanding when to use each one help support children's decoding and spelling skills. Teach them this mnemonic to help them remember this order: *The cat kissed the duck.*

/k/ Spelled -*ck* Words

-ack			
back	**rack**	**knack**	**smack**
hack	sack	quack	snack
Jack	**tack**	**shack**	stack
lack	black	**slack**	track
pack	crack		

-eck			
deck	neck	check	**speck**
heck	**peck**	**fleck**	**wreck**

-ick			
Dick	Rick	chick	**slick**
kick	sick	click	stick
lick	tick	**flick**	thick
Nick	**wick**	quick	trick
pick	brick		

-ock			
dock	sock	**crock**	shock
lock	**tock**	**flock**	**smock**
mock	block	knock	**stock**
rock	clock		

-uck			
buck	**puck**	Chuck	struck
duck	**suck**	cluck	stuck
luck	tuck	**pluck**	truck
muck	yuck	snuck	

/k/ Spelled -ck Phrases

flock of ducks	black socks	truck got stuck
rack of socks	black truck	slick dock
sack of rocks	a chick and a duck	stick his neck out
tick tock	crack on the clock	lock the shack
thick block	a stick and a rock	snack on the deck
muck on the dock	track the duck	locket in her pocket
can crack the nut	a small wick	quick as a bunny
on the stick	a speck of dust	will stack the blocks
on the big deck	stack of red bricks	hangs on a rack

/k/ **Spelled** -*ck* Sentences

Run on the track.	The duck is quick.
A duck is stuck in the muck.	The clock had a crack.
The ducks said quack.	Take some snacks on the hike.
The chick said cluck.	Smack the rock with the stick.
A chick and a duck hung out.	Pick up the rack of socks.
Nick will kick the rock.	We had a snack on the deck.
Tick tock went the clock.	Lock up the bike at the dock.
Pick up the stick and rock.	Dad packs the best snacks.
Check on the baby chicks.	Do not stick your neck out.
Jack sat on the deck.	Check the lock on the bike.
The chicks can rest on the stick.	Stack the blocks on the deck.
A fleck of dust landed on the rock.	Jack ate a snack on the brick wall.
It's just my luck to get stuck in the muck.	A flock of ducks swam to the dock.
The clock went click clack and broke.	The black truck got stuck in the muck.

-ke vs. -ck

Use the lists below to contrast the /k/ endings -ke (which follows a long vowel, as in *lake*) with -ck (which often follows a short vowel, as in *lack*).

-ke vs. -ck Words

-ke	-ck
bake	back
Jake	Jack
lake	lack
like	lick
Mike	Mick
pike	pick
poke	pock
rake	rack
sake	sack
take	tack
choke	chock
flake	flack
quake	quack
shake	shack
snake	snack
stake	stack
trike	trick

-*ke* vs. -*ck* Phrases

can pick the rake	feel the shack shake	poke with a stick
likes her trick	shakes in the shack	can stack the sticks
will pick up a pike	like and lick the cake	lack of bikes
hike with a backpack	take some snacks	will take a pack

-*ke* vs. -*ck* Sentences

Nell will take some snacks.	Pick up pike to bake.
Take the tack off the seat.	Put the bike on the rack.
I will take my backpack.	Bring the cake back to bake.
Pick up the rake in the back.	Feed the snake some snacks.
I like her card tricks.	Pack a snack in the sack.
Len likes to lick the cake.	Mike is back with a cake.
Jane is back home.	Shelly can feel the shack shake.
You can stack the sticks in the back.	We had a snack with a nice snake.

Consonant *x*

The letter *x* commonly appears at the end of words and is pronounced /ks/. The final *x* might be confused with a word that ends with *-ck + s* (e.g., *tax* vs. *tacks*).

Consonant *x* Words

box	**lox**	**tax**	**flex**
fax	Max	**tux**	next
fix	mix	**vex**	mailbox
fox	sax	wax	relax
lax	six	**flax**	remix

Consonant *x* Phrases

fox in a box	six boxes	can fix the sax
fox in a tux	will mix the wax	next to the mailbox
can mix a cake	five or six	can relax in bed

Consonant *x* Sentences

The fox sat in the box.	Relax and listen to the sax.
Take five or six boxes.	Mix the cake well.
Please fix the mailbox.	The fax is close to the exit.
Don't vex the fox.	Max looks good in a tux.
Play the sax in a tux.	Fix the wax on the box.
Six foxes got into six boxes.	There is a box next to the mailbox.

Consonant *qu*

In English words, the letter *q* often appears with *u*. Together, they are pronounced /kw/.

Consonant *qu* Words

quid	**quest**	**quart**	**squat**
quip	quilt	quarter	**squid**
quit	**quail**	question	squint
quiz	**quaint**	quiet	squish
quack	queen	**quiver**	square
quick	quite	**quokka**	**squawk**
quill	**quote**		

Consonant *qu* Phrases

a fun quest	a quill pen	a quiet room
queen's quilt	queen's quote	quick quiz
quiver of quills	quaint quilt	quiz about quotes
a long squid	quilt square	the quiet queen

Consonant *qu* Sentences

The queen loves to quilt.	The king loves the queen.
He squats next to the quail.	I have a quick question.
Have you seen a quokka?	The quilt was quite quaint.
The squid is quite long.	The queen has a quiver of quills.
The queen went on a quest to find quails.	How many questions are in the quiz?
One quarter is the same as 25 cents.	The quiz about quotes is quite hard.

Consonant *w*

The /w/ sound is pronounced by forming a tight circle with your lips and pushing forward to release the sound. When the letter *a* follows *w*, as in *water*, it has a variable sound.

Consonant *w* Words

wag	well	wing	wore
was	will	wish	work
wax	want	with	worm
web	**wend**	wake	wool
wed	**west**	woke	wild
wet	**wilt**	wait	were
wig	wind	way	walnut
win	**wisp**	warm	walrus
wit	wash	wart	water
wall	watch	word	wonder

Consonant *w* Phrases

wet wool	wish for some wings	work and win
wet cobweb	warm wall	wax wings
west wind	will be well	warm water
with the wind	wag and wag	walruses in water
a wild wind	wild worms	wild walruses
wisp of wind	soap and water to wash	can wash with warm water

Consonant *w* Sentences

Wax the van.	Will woke up late.
I want to make a wish.	The wind made it hard to win.
The bird's wing was wide.	Make a wonderful wish.
Will is on his way home.	They can win the word game.
The water comes from the well.	Drink lots of water on a hot day.
The ant got stuck in the web.	Wax the car for your dad.
We woke up to a warm wind.	Watch out for wild walnuts.
Swab the decks with water.	The flowers will wilt if it is warm.
Watch where the walnuts fall.	Wait and all will be well.
The wet wig was in the sun.	Dogs want to wag their tails.
Wind the sheep's wool.	Waxwings are a kind of bird.
The wispy cobwebs were sticky.	Wings made of wax might melt.
Wash with soap and water.	We went west with the wind.
After the storm, the car was wet.	I want to wake up late on Wednesday.
The west wind swept over the wall.	The cobwebs were on the west wall.
Will, the walrus, lives in the west.	Use soap and water to wash the wig.

Consonant y

As a consonant, the letter *y* often appears at the beginning of a word or syllable. The /y/ sound is pronounced by raising the sides of the tongue against the upper teeth. The lips are stretched from side to side when making the sound.

Consonant y Words

yak	yum	**yeast**	your
yam	yup	yard	yellow
yap	yell	yarn	yo-yo
yen	yuck	yawn	**yodel**
yes	yank	**yowl**	yoga
yet	**yoke**	**yolk**	yummy
yip	year	you	yesterday

Consonant y Phrases

yip and yap	yodel and yell	year of the yak
yes not yup	yummy yams	yellow yarn
yank the yo-yo	yawn and yowl	yum or yuck
yes or no	an egg yolk	you and me
in yoga class	a ball of yarn	not yet

Consonant y Sentences

Don't yell at the yak.	The sun is yellow.
Did you say yes?	Yams are yum, not yuck.
Say yes, not yup.	Don't yodel during yoga.
I saw you yawn.	The yaks began to yodel and yell.
Yesterday, yaks came into our yard.	The hat was made with yellow yarn.

Double Final Consonants: *Floss*

"Floss" is a spelling pattern we often introduce to young learners. In a one-syllable word with a short vowel followed by *f, l,* or *s* (and sometimes *z*), the final consonant is usually doubled. English words do not typically end with a single *s* pronounced /s/. However, when a word does end in a single *s*, such as *bus* or *gas,* its spelling is due to its word origin. A mnemonic to remember the letters is: *Fuzzy zebras sip lemonade.*

Floss Words

-ff			
buff	off	**cliff**	sniff
cuff	puff	fluff	staff
huff	**riff**	**gruff**	stiff
miff	**tiff**	**scoff**	stuff
muff	**bluff**	**scuff**	**whiff**
-ll			
ball	fall	Jill	sell
bell	fell	**lull**	**sill**
bill	fill	mall	tall
bull	full	**mill**	tell
call	**gall**	**mull**	till
cell	**gill**	**null**	**toll**
cull	gull	**pall**	wall
dell	hall	pill	well
dill	hill	pull	will
doll	**hull**	**rill**	yell
dull	ill	roll	chill

-ll continued			
drill	**quell**	skill	spill
frill	**quill**	small	stall
grill	shall	smell	still
krill	shell	spell	**swell**
-ss			
bass	less	toss	dress
Bess	loss	**bliss**	floss
boss	**mass**	brass	glass
fuss	mess	**chess**	**gloss**
hiss	miss	class	grass
kiss	**moss**	**cress**	press
lass	pass	cross	**Swiss**
-zz			
buzz	fuzz	jazz	frizz
fizz			

Floss Phrases

grass on the cliff	chill on the hill	moss on the hill
huff and puff	skill with a quill	jazz class
fluff and stuff	fluff on the dress	can smell the mess
fuzz and fizz	can spell with skill	will buzz the bell
miss the train	catch and pass	chess class
still wants to yell	on the grass	can hear the jazz
a new red dress	krill in a shell	a fun class

Floss Sentences

There is grass on the cliff.	The bell is set to buzz.
Biff can spell with skill.	Fish eat krill, but not with dill.
Did the wolf huff and puff?	Fill the cup with dill.
Huff and puff up the hill.	The moss on the hill is soft.
Don't fall on the slick grass.	The kids spell with skill.
We shall have fun in jazz class.	The grass on the cliff is long.
There was fluff and stuff on my dress.	The jazz class will play on the hill.
Let's chill on the moss on the hill.	The drink began to fuzz and fizz.
Press the bell to start the chess class.	I can smell the mess, but don't make a fuss.

s-Blends

Consonant clusters, also known as *consonant blends*, are two consonants that appear next to each other but keep their individual sounds when blended. You might tell children that consonant blends are friends that hang out together, but each has its own voice. Blends can be challenging for early readers and spellers who may delete one of the consonant sounds.

s-Blend Words

sc-			
scab	scale	**scar**	scoot
scan	scare	scarf	scooter
scat	**scope**	**scout**	scuba
scold	score	scoop	

sk-			
skid	skip	**sketch**	ski
skim	**skit**	skunk	sky
skin	skill	skate	skirt

sm-			
smog	small	smoke	**smooth**
smug	smell	smart	**smudge**
smash	smile		

sn-			
snap	snack	snore	sneeze
snip	**sniff**	snail	snout
snob	snake	**sneak**	snow
snug			

sp-			
span	spend	**spare**	sport
spat	spent	speak	**spur**
spin	spill	**spear**	spoil
spit	space	spy	spoon
spot	**spine**	**spar**	

st-			
stag	still	stare	steal
stem	stamp	state	steel
step	stand	stone	**steep**
stop	sting	store	star
stack	stink	stove	start
stick	**stitch**	**stain**	stir
stock	**stomp**	stair	storm
stuck	stage	stay	stew
staff	**stake**	steak	story
stall	**stale**		

sw-			
swam	**swell**	swing	sweep
swan	**swamp**	swish	sweet
swap	swept	**switch**	sweat
swat	**swift**	sway	**swoop**
swim			

s-Blend Phrases

stop and start	smell or sniff	scab on my skin
snug in the snow	will step on the snow	spy with skill
smog and smoke	steep stairs	sticks and stones
can smell the skunk	will stare at the stag	can stitch the scarf
speedy scooter	stars in space	smile and speak

s-Blend Sentences

Stop and step over the stones.	Stop and start and skip.
Snip and snap the stems.	They are snug in the snow cave.
I like the smell of skim milk.	We can smell the smoke.
Don't swim in the swell.	The swan swam away.
Smell the fresh snow.	Stomp on the stack of sticks.
The smug spy has skills.	Look at all the stars in the sky.
Can you smell the skunk?	Step and stomp on the snow.
I can see the stars in space.	Stick a stamp on the card.
The skunk stunk up our stuff.	She can skate with skill.
Stack the sticks next to the stones.	Don't skid on your speedy scooter.
Stella can stitch the scarf with yarn.	The scab on my skin is from a fall.

r-Blends

Some children may find *r*-blends difficult to pronounce. You might have children first say the individual consonants in isolation, /b/ /r/, and then together, /br/, as in *brush*. Having a folding card with the blends on one side and words on the other is also helpful. The blends *tr* and *dr* are commonly misspelled as *jr* or *chr* due to how similarly they are articulated.

r-Blend Words

br-			
brag	**broth**	**brain**	**brew**
bran	brush	**bray**	**broad**
brim	branch	break	broil
brand	brunch	breathe	brook
brass	**brave**	breeze	broom
brick	bride	bright	brown
brash	**brine**	bread	brought
bridge	broke	breath	brother
bring	braid		
cr-			
crab	**crept**	**crate**	crow
cram	**crest**	creak	cry
crib	crumb	cream	crawl
crop	crust	creek	**crook**
crack	crash	creep	**crouch**
craft	crunch	cried	crowd
cross	**crane**	**croak**	crown

dr-			
drab	dress	**drake**	drain
drag	**drill**	**drape**	dream
drip	**drift**	drive	draw
drop	drank	drove	drew
drum	drink	dry	**dread**

fr-			
frog	**frost**	frame	friend
frill	Frank	free	fruit
frizz	**fresh**	**freeze**	from
front	**French**	**fright**	

gr-			
grab	**gruff**	**graze**	grow
gram	grand	**grime**	grown
grid	**grasp**	**gripe**	grew
grim	grump	grain	groom
grin	**graph**	gray	**grouch**
grip	grace	great	ground
grit	grade	greed	group
grub	grape	green	growl
grass	**grate**	greet	
grill	**grave**	groan	

pr-			
pram	press	prize	**prance**
prim	print	prune	prince
prod	price	**pry**	**proof**
prop	**pride**	pray	proud

tr-			
trap	truck	trade	**troop**
trek	troll	trail	**true**
trim	tramp	train	**truth**
trip	**trust**	tray	**tread**
trot	trash	treat	trough
track	trunk	tree	trout
trick	trace	try	

r-Blend Phrases

brave frog	fresh crab	bread or bran
the crab and frog	didn't drop the drum	truck trade
broth at brunch	trip in the truck	can bring some fruit
brown grass	prunes the branch	will grill some trout
greets her brother	grim troll	fruit and cream
can bring the bread	freeze frame	green frog
Pru the princess	cry croak, croak	a treat on the tray
prince's crown	will press the dress	bridge made of brick

r-Blend Sentences

Crash went the drum.	Don't trust Prince Frank.
We had fresh crab for brunch.	I hear a cry from the crib.
Brad loves to eat bran.	Brenda brushes her long braid.
Pru is a proud princess.	Let's trek to see the trees.
The crab has a crack in its shell.	Drew loves to draw and dream.
A drip of broth fell on her dress.	Never try to trick Trent.
There is frost on the fresh fruit.	She hang her wet dress to dry.
The crab and frog are best friends.	The grim troll hid under the bridge.
Drink the broth and eat some bread.	The brash brothers began to brag.
The trip in the truck was a long drive.	The broth at brunch dripped on her dress.
Don't cram crumbs into your mouth.	The brave frog went crash into the pond.
The white cranes land next to the creek.	We creep and crawl to the crest of the hill.
I cut off the crust on the crunchy toast.	Does a crab or a frog say "croak"?
The truck bed was full of tree branches.	It isn't great that trash fell out of the truck.

l-Blends

Some children may find *l*-blends difficult to pronounce due to the consonant *l* being part of the blend cluster. These blends take practice. You might have children first say the individual consonants in isolation, /s/ /l/, and then together, /sl/, as in *sled*. Having a folding card with the blends on one side and words on the other is also helpful.

l-Blend Words

bl-			
blab	block	blush	blind
bled	**bluff**	**blade**	blow
blip	blast	**blame**	blew
blob	blend	blaze	blood
blot	blond	bleach	bloom
black	blank	**bleat**	blouse
bless	blink	bleed	

cl-			
clad	click	**cling**	climb
clam	clock	cloth	**cloak**
clan	cluck	**clutch**	**clerk**
clap	class	close	claw
clip	**cliff**	**claim**	cloud
clod	clamp	clay	clown
clog	**clump**	clean	clue
clop	clang	clear	
club	**clash**	**cleat**	

fl–			
flag	flock	**flake**	flight
flap	floss	flame	float
flat	fluff	**flare**	flow
flip	flash	**fluke**	**flaw**
flit	**flesh**	flute	flew
flop	flush	flu	**flood**
flub	fling	fly	floor
fleck	flung	**flea**	flour
flick	**flunk**	**fleet**	

gl–			
glad	**gloss**	**glide**	glow
glib	**glance**	globe	glue
glob	**glitch**	**gleam**	**gloom**
glum	**glare**	**glee**	glove
glass	**glaze**	**gloat**	

pl–			
plan	plum	place	play
plod	**plus**	plane	**plead**
plop	plant	plate	please
plot	**plank**	plaid	**pleat**
plug	**plush**	**plain**	**plow**

sl–			
slab	slob	**slump**	sleep
slam	**slop**	slush	**sleet**
slap	**slot**	**slate**	sleeve
sled	slug	slice	slight
slid	slack	slide	**sly**
slim	**slick**	slime	slow
slip	**slant**	slope	**slaw**
slit	slept	sleek	

l-Blend Phrases

club at the cliff	plans to eat plums	slop or slime
black block	flip and flop	slid on the slush
clod of clay	clip and clop	plush plum
flicks the flea	blows the flute	fly flew away
can place the glass	cleaned his plate	clear clue
a glum clown	fleet of planes	went to sleep

l-Blend Sentences

The flag will flap in the wind.	The club met at the cliff.
You can be glad or glum.	The fluff gets flat when wet.
I saw clowns climb the cliff.	We slid in the slush and slime.
Will the block float?	We plan to eat plums.
Can a clam clap?	The plane flew across the globe.
Slow down so the sled doesn't slip.	There are many flags all over the globe.

Tri-Blends

Tri-blends, or three-letter blends, are three consonants that are coarticulated. They all contain an *s* and either an *l* or *r*. Some children find tri-blends challenging to pronounce when reading. Children sometimes do not include all three sounds when spelling a word. To provide practice reading and spelling words with tri-blends, have children coarticulate and spell these tri-blends in isolation and then respectively in words.

Tri-Blends Words

scr-			
scram	**scrum**	**scratch**	screen
scrap	**script**	scrape	**scrawl**
scrub	**scroll**	scream	screw

spl-			
splat	split	**splint**	splash

spr-			
sprig	spring	**sprain**	**sprawl**
sprint	sprung	spray	**sprout**
sprang	**spruce**	**spry**	

str-			
strap	**strict**	**strike**	**stray**
strip	stretch	stripe	**streak**
strum	string	**stroke**	stream
stress	strong	**straight**	street
struck	**strung**	**strain**	straw
strand	**stride**	**strange**	**stroll**

Tri-Blends Phrases

spring sprang	splish-splash	split splint
strong string	sprigs of green	rip in the screen
stretch up and up	across the street	a sprig of mint
yellow straw	sprouts in the grass	kite string
spruce trees	stroke of luck	yawn and stretch
sprouts of green sprung	scratch on the screen	stroll next to the stream

Tri-Blends Sentences

Don't scrap the script.	The spry man can sprint fast.
Stretch the string very long.	Splat, the fruit split in half.
The string is very strong.	Spring has sprung.
There is a scratch on the screen.	Yawn and stretch and touch the sky.
Spring sprang and all was green.	A sprout sprung from the ground.
We see sprigs of green in the spring.	The stress on the string made it snap.
Scrub the screen to make it clean.	Splish-splash, we are in the bath.
The kite string got stuck in the tree.	Pick up the cones from the spruce tree.
The cat can stretch and play with string.	Let's cross the street and stroll by the stream.

Final Blends

Final blends are letters that commonly appear together at the end of words. As with initial blends, each letter has its own sound, but they are coarticulated. Final blends can be challenging for early readers and spellers who may delete one of the consonant sounds.

Final Blends Words

-ct			
act	fact	strict	tract
duct	pact		

-ft			
gift	loft	soft	drift
heft	raft	cleft	swift
left	rift	craft	shaft
lift	sift	draft	shift

-lk			
bulk	milk	sulk	whelk
elk	silk		

-lp			
alp	help	pulp	scalp
gulp	kelp	yelp	

-lt			
belt	pelt	bolt	built
felt	salt	colt	guilt
halt	tilt	jolt	quilt
kilt	welt	fault	
melt	wilt		

-mp			
amp	limp	cramp	swamp
bump	lump	crimp	tramp
camp	pump	grump	trump
damp	ramp	plump	champ
dump	romp	skimp	chimp
hump	blimp	slump	shrimp
jump	clamp	stamp	thump
lamp	clump	stomp	

-nd			
and	pond	spend	ground
band	sand	stand	friend
bend	send	strand	bind
bond	tend	trend	find
end	wand	found	hind
fond	wind	hound	kind
fund	bland	mound	mind
hand	blend	pound	rind
land	blond	round	blind
lend	brand	sound	grind
mend	grand	wound	

-nt			
ant	lent	tent	print
bent	**lint**	**tint**	scent
bunt	mint	**vent**	spent
cent	pant	want	**splint**
dent	**punt**	went	split
font	rent	front	**faint**
hint	**runt**	**grant**	paint
hunt	sent	plant	**pint**

-pt			
apt	**rapt**	slept	swept
kept	**wept**		

-sk			
ask	**dusk**	**musk**	**tusk**
bask	husk	risk	brisk
desk	mask	**task**	**whisk**
disk			

-sp			
gasp	**wisp**	crisp	**grasp**
wasp	**clasp**		

-st			
best	last	rust	**boast**
bust	list	test	**coast**
cast	lost	vest	**east**
cost	**mast**	**west**	feast
dust	mist	**zest**	least
fast	must	blast	roast
fist	nest	chest	toast
gust	past	**quest**	ghost
jest	**pest**	twist	most
just	rest	wrist	post

Final Blends Phrases

will hunt for facts	milk in bulk	mask with tusks
bump and jump	will gulp the pulp	went at dusk
pact to act	lamp on the desk	quest for a chest
will paint the ramp	brisk wind	best friend
lost colt	acts like a champ	round mound
last stand	camp in a tent	damp ground
a raft with heft	a ramp to the pond	mist in the west
a kind gift	a vest for camp	a draft in the wind
will post the list	on a quest with zest	west of the coast

Final Blends Sentences

The facts that are left can help.	The raft was a gift.
I felt I could melt in the sun.	My best friend gave me a gift.
A wasp made her gasp.	Don't gulp the pulp in the drink.
The band was very grand.	He slept after he swept.
We went on an ant hunt.	The ground was damp at dusk.
Don't clasp or grasp a wasp.	We made a pact to act soon.
Let's jump with zest.	There is a mound in the ground.
She swept lint under the rug.	Pitch a tent next to the pond.
When she wins, she acts like a champ.	We found the lost colt next to the post.
They got milk in bulk at the store.	It would be good to have a lamp at camp.
Find the band next to the stand.	The mask with tusks was on the desk.
Paint the mask for arts and crafts.	A whelk shell was next to the kelp.
We went on a quest for a chest of gold.	The boat mast might rust in the mist.

Flexing Grid (VC, CVC, CCVC)

A flexing grid is a useful exercise for children when first learning to read consonant blends. Have children follow across each row, left to right, shifting from a VC (vowel-consonant) word to a CVC word to a CCVC word; for example, *id* to *lid* to *slid*. You may wish to include nonsense words in a flexing grid.

Sample Word List

VC	CVC	CCVC
ab	lab	slab
ad	lad	glad
am	ram	tram
an	can	scan
ap	lap	flap
ed	led	sled
id	lid	slid
in	pin	spin
it	lit	flit
ob	lob	blob
op	top	stop
ot	lot	plot
ub	rub	grub
ug	lug	slug

Digraph *sh*

Consonant digraphs are two consonants that appear next to each other but represent one sound. Digraphs commonly include an *h*.

Digraph *sh* Words

sh (initial position)			
shad	shell	shape	shy
sham	shelf	share	shark
shed	**shift**	shave	sharp
shin	shred	shine	shirt
ship	**shrill**	shore	short
shop	shrub	**shrine**	**shawl**
shot	shrug	she	shoe
shun	shrimp	sheep	shoot
shut	shrink	**sheer**	**shrew**
shack	shade	sheet	should
shock	shake	**shield**	
shall	shame	show	

sh (final position)			
ash	dish	hush	**mesh**
bash	fish	Josh	**mush**
bush	**gash**	lash	push
cash	**gush**	**lush**	**rash**
dash	**hash**	mash	rush

sh continued			
sash	clash	**quash**	splash
wash	crash	shush	squash
wish	crush	slush	trash
blush	flash	smash	**leash**
brush	fresh		
sh (compound words)			
fishbone	horseshoe	starfish	washcloth
hairbrush	jellyfish	sunshine	wishbone

Digraph sh Phrases

shy sheep	fish on the ship	will show your shoe
fish on a dish	fish shop	shipshape
shell on the shore	rash on my shin	cash in the dish
wash the shirt	splash on the shore	in the shade
dash to the shack	short on cash	shut the shed
mush in the trash	shark with jellyfish	crash and smash
will shop for a shawl	short shelf	can mash the hash
shack in the shade	was hit in the shin	mush on a dish
sheep on a ship	fresh shrimp	starfish on the sand

Digraph *sh* Sentences

There are fish in the shed.	The hash on the plate is mush.
Make a wish for a fish.	Rush to the fish shop.
Bring cash to the fish shop.	Let's rush to dash to the ship.
The sheep are on the ship.	Hush, don't wake the fish.
Make a wish and you will shine!	The rash on my shin is red.
Splash into the tub to wash.	Wash the shrimp and fish.
The shack is in the shade.	Shep was hit in the shin.
Rush to the ship.	The mush is in the trash.
A starfish lay on the sand.	Put the fishbones in the trash.
Sit and rest in the shade.	A fish sat on a dish.
The shells lay on the shore.	Shop for fresh fish.
Dash to the shack and back.	The shell sat on the shelf.
The sheep are in the shed.	The shrub grew by the bush.
The fish on the dish is from the ship.	Crush the trash to take to the dump.
We need shade from the sunshine.	The sunshine is going to flash brightly.
All is shipshape and set to shine.	You can plant the shrub in the shade.

Digraph *th*

The digraph *th* has an unvoiced sound, as in *thin,* and a voiced sound, as in *that.* The sound /th/ is formed by sticking your tongue between your teeth. It can be confused with /f/, in which the upper teeth rest on the lower lip.

Digraph *th* Words

th (unvoiced, initial position)			
thin	thing	**thief**	thirst
thud	think	three	thorn
thug	thumb	throw	thought
thick	thump	**thaw**	thread
theft	**theme**	third	through
thank			
th (unvoiced, final position)			
bath	**broth**	tenth	**north**
Beth	cloth	**growth**	**worth**
both	fifth	**oath**	**booth**
math	**froth**	teeth	death
moth	**length**	**wreath**	mouth
path	sixth	birth	**south**
with	**sloth**	fourth	tooth
th (voiced, initial position)			
than	then	those	their
that	this	they	there
them	these	though	the
th (compound words)			
bathtub	dishcloth	**withheld**	

Digraph *th* Phrases

thin sloth	with a thud	tenth of the length
moth in the bath	thin broth	thick froth
think math	thick and thin	thud and thump
this and that	sloth went south	then turn north
fourth tooth	both teeth	this thread
moth flew north	will thank Beth	length of cloth

Digraph *th* Sentences

The sloth got lost on the path.	The moth flew north.
The thin broth did not froth.	We think math is fun.
The thin cloth can rip.	It is fun to sip the thick froth.
He lost his fourth tooth.	A tenth of the path is mud.
The sloth fell with a thud.	Seth did three math problems.
Seth lost both teeth.	Rip the thread from the shirt.
Cut a long length of cloth.	The sloth went north and then south.
What fell with a thud and a thump?	How many teeth are in your mouth?
Seth fell into the bath with a thud.	They were chums through thick and thin.
Moths in the bath is not a good thing.	Beth and Seth went on this path.

Digraph *wh*

The digraph *wh* often appears in question words (such as *who* and *what*) and "noise" words (such as *whiz* and *whir*). This digraph represents the /w/ sound and less commonly, the /hw/ sound.

Digraph *wh* Words

wham	**whack**	whine	why
what	**whiff**	white	where
when	**whisk**	wheat	**whir**
whim	which	wheel	**whirl**
whip	whale	whew	
whiz	while	**whey**	

Digraph *wh* Phrases

white whale	on a whim	wide wheel
white snow	wheel on a bike	not sure why
whiz and wham	catch a whiff	whiz kid
whisk the egg white	which wheel	when and where

Digraph *wh* Sentences

Whit is a whiz at math.	The whale can hear a whine.
When will we get there?	Please don't whine.
Where did the white whale swim to?	The white whale whacked its tail.
The wide wheels make the truck whiz along.	We went on a whale watch on a whim.
Which whale did you see at the beach?	Whip and whisk up the birthday cake.

Digraph *ph*

The digraph *ph* is one of the spellings for the /f/ sound. This Greek digraph is commonly taught later because the words are often more advanced multisyllabic words.

Digraph *ph* Words

ph (initial position)			
phone	phonics	photo	**phrase**
ph (final position)			
graph	photograph	**triumph**	
ph (medial position)			
dolphin	**hyphen**	**orphan**	telephone
elephant	nephew	**symphony**	trophy

Digraph *ph* Phrases

on the phone	short phrase	dolphins and whales
lines on a graph	black and white photo	won a trophy

Digraph *ph* Sentences

I like black and white photos.	They won a trophy.
Phil was on the phone for a long time.	Write a short phrase about the photo.
The lines on the graph go up and down.	Dolphins and whales play in the sea.

Digraphs *ch, -tch*

The /ch/ sound can be represented by *ch* or *-tch*. When /ch/ comes at the end of a word, commonly after the letter *n* or an *r*-controlled vowel, it is spelled *ch*, as in *lunch* or *porch*. When /ch/ comes at the end of a one-syllable word right after a short vowel, it is commonly spelled *-tch*, as in *patch*. Since the *t* in *-tch* is silent, both spellings—*ch* and *-tch*—are pronounced the same. No English word begins with *-tch*.

Digraph *ch, -tch* Words

ch (initial position)			
chap	Chuck	change	child
chat	**chess**	chase	chair
chin	chill	**chime**	charm
chip	champ	chose	chart
chop	chant	chain	chirp
chug	chest	cheap	chalk
chum	chimp	cheat	chew
check	chomp	cheep	choose
chick	**chunk**	cheese	**chow**
ch (final position)			
much	lunch	crunch	peach
rich	munch	**drench**	reach
such	pinch	grinch	teach
which	punch	**quench**	**arch**
bench	ranch	**stench**	**birch**
bunch	branch	**trench**	**perch**
finch	church	scrunch	couch
hunch	**clench**	beach	search
inch	**clinch**	each	touch

-tch (final position)			
batch	hatch	pitch	snatch
botch	**hutch**	watch	**splotch**
catch	itch	witch	stitch
ditch	match	**blotch**	**swatch**
etch	**notch**	scratch	switch
fetch	patch	sketch	**twitch**

Digraph *ch, -tch* Phrases

chips at lunch	pinch on the chin	bunch of change
chat with the chap	chess champ	hatch some chicks
chill on the beach	reach into the chest	munch and crunch
crunch some chips	munch on cheese	will watch the child
stitch and patch	in a ditch	notch in the branch
sketch of a witch	will hatch a plan	pitch and catch
can scratch the itch	splotch or blotch	which witch
pitch like a champ	check your watch	a branch in the ditch
stitch an inch	will fetch the branch	hunch about the hutch

Digraph *ch, -tch* Sentences

I like to crunch on chips.	Munch on cheese at the ranch.
That chap is my chum.	The chess champ had a hunch.
Let us chat with a chimp.	Did the chicks hatch yet?
Stitch and patch the top.	Pitch the ball, and I will catch it.
The dog will fetch the stick.	Watch the child at the beach.
Don't scratch the itch.	There is a notch in the branch.
Mitch fell in the ditch.	The stitch is an inch long.
The finch sat on a branch.	Sketch the arch over the hutch.
Pinch an inch off the next batch.	How many chips can you crunch?
Chat with the chap about the match.	Check before you chop the branch.
The finch can perch on the arch.	The catcher and pitcher are on the same team.
Let's chill on the bench with our chums.	Please don't pinch me on the chin.

Welded Ending -*ng*

The sound /ng/ is often represented by the letters *ng* and often comes at the end of a word or syllable. It is easiest to decode when attached to a vowel: *-ang, -ing, -ong, -ung*. It is never attached to an *e*.

Welded Ending -*ng* Words

-ang			
bang	hang	sang	**slang**
fang	**pang**	**tang**	**twang**
gang	rang	**clang**	

-ing			
ding	wing	fling	string
king	**zing**	sling	swing
ping	**bling**	spring	thing
ring	bring	sting	**wring**
sing	**cling**		

-ong			
gong	song	strong	ping-pong
long	**tong**	wrong	

-ung			
dung	rung	flung	stung
hung	sung	**slung**	swung
lung	**clung**	sprung	young

Welded Ending *-ng* Phrases

long song	king on a swing	will play ping-pong
slang with a twang	king in a sling	long fang
king with a ring	will bring the sling	cling to the swing
clang of the gong	thing with wings	ring ding-a-ling
arm in a sling	strong tongs	with a bang
will fling the string	hung a gong	got stung

Welded Ending *-ng* Sentences

The long song went on and on.	He rang the gong.
The king sat on the swing.	Bang went the gong.
The king had a gold ring.	He rang the bell.
Bring the sling for the king.	The thing went zing.
The bell rang and rang.	The snake had long fangs.
The king got stung.	Hang the bell with a long string.
She sang slang with a twang.	Don't play ping-pong with tongs.
Birds love to sing in the spring.	The drink had a strong tang.
Stan got stung by a bee.	Pam flung the ping-pong ball.
A bug bite can sting for a long time.	They hung the gong on the branch.

Welded Ending *-nk*

The sound /ngk/ is often represented by the letters *nk*. Like /ng/, the sound /ngk/ is also easiest to decode when attached to a vowel: *-ank, -ink, -onk, -unk*. It is never attached to an *e*.

Welded Ending *-nk* Words

-ank			
bank	sank	**crank**	**plank**
dank	tank	drank	**prank**
Hank	**yank**	**flank**	**stank**
lank	blank	Frank	thank
rank	clank		

-ink			
ink	rink	**brink**	**slink**
link	sink	**clink**	stink
mink	wink	drink	think
pink	blink		

-onk			
bonk	**conk**	honk	

-unk			
bunk	**hunk**	**flunk**	**slunk**
dunk	junk	**plunk**	**spunk**
funk	sunk	shrunk	stunk
gunk	**clunk**	skunk	trunk

Welded Ending *-nk* Phrases

pink skunk	wink and blink	yank the trunk
skunk with spunk	sunk junk	under the bunk
junk trunk	drank the drink	gunk on the trunk
will thank Hank	in the bank	a pink drink
clink, clank, clunk	hunk of junk	can drink in the sink
can pack a trunk	plays a prank	will sink in the tank

Welded Ending *-nk* Sentences

The pink skunk hid in the trunk.	He drank the pink drink.
Slink into the rink to skate.	Thank you for the pink trunk.
The trunk is full of junk.	The prank made the room stink.
Did you wink or blink?	Write in ink in the blank book.
The junk sunk next to the dock.	Turn the crank for a prank.
Dunk the cookie in the drink.	I have a pink piggy bank.
That trunk is a hunk of junk.	Wink at the pink skunk.
Clink, clank, clunk, went the junk.	The skunk began to shrink.
The rock sank in the fish tank.	I think the ink is red.
Yank the trunk from under the bunk.	The skunk stunk but has much spunk.

Welded Endings -*ng* and -*nk*

The digraph -*ng* and the blend -*nk* are easiest to decode when they are attached to a vowel. They are never attached to the vowel *e*.

Mixed -*ng* and -*nk* Phrases

eyes sting	the pink thing	skunk can sing
pink ping-pong	wink and sing	long plank
ink on the swing	pink string	thing in the sink
the junk ring	king in a funk	strong trunk
Hank the king	clink and clang	can bring a drink
string in a trunk	ring in a sink	Ming the mink

Mixed -*ng* and -*nk* Sentences

The stink made my eyes sting.	The king can sing in the sink.
We had pink ping-pong balls.	Hank can hang from the swing.
Think about the thing I said.	The king's swing had a kink.
Clink and clunk rang the gong.	Oh, no! The skunk got stung!
Bring me a pink drink.	Please don't yank the wings.
Does a duck sing "honk-honk"?	The trunk is full of string.
Ming the mink can sing.	The thing in the sink stinks.
Can a skunk sing a song?	The king is in a funk.
Hank can wink and sing at the same time.	The ducks had to walk on a long plank.

Final e (VCe)

In the vowel-consonant-e (VCe) pattern, the final e (sometimes referred to as "silent e") makes the vowel long. Only one consonant separates the vowel from the final e. In *u_e* words, the *u* has two sounds: /ū/, as in *mule*, and /o͞o/, as in *rule*. Note: e_e is not common in a one-syllable word.

Final e Words

a_e			
ace	**gale**	mane	same
age	game	**mate**	**sane**
ate	**gape**	maze	save
bake	gate	name	take
base	gave	**pace**	tale
cake	hate	**pale**	**tame**
came	**haze**	pane	tape
cane	**jade**	**pave**	**vane**
cape	**kale**	race	vase
case	lake	**rage**	**wade**
cave	**lame**	rake	wake
date	lane	**rale**	**wane**
daze	late	rate	wave
face	**laze**	**rave**	**blade**
fade	made	safe	**blame**
fake	make	**sake**	**blaze**
fame	male	sale	**brace**

a_e continued			
brake	frame	plate	**slate**
brave	**glade**	quake	snake
chase	**glaze**	scale	space
crane	**grace**	scrape	**spade**
crate	grade	shade	stage
craze	grape	shake	**stake**
drake	**grate**	shame	stale
drape	**grave**	shape	trace
flake	place	shave	**trade**
flame	plane	skate	whale
e_e			
eke	Pete	**theme**	these
Eve	Steve		
i_e			
bike	hide	lime	pine
bite	hike	line	pipe
dice	hive	live	rice
dime	ice	mice	ride
dine	kite	mile	**ripe**
file	**lice**	mine	rise
fine	life	nine	side
five	like	pile	tide

i_e continued			
tile	**brine**	quite	strike
time	chime	shine	stripe
vine	**chive**	slice	**swine**
wide	crime	slide	twice
wife	drive	slime	**twine**
wipe	glide	smile	while
wise	price	**spike**	whine
bribe	pride	**spine**	white
bride	prize	**stride**	write

o_e			
bone	**mole**	woke	quote
code	**mope**	**zone**	**scone**
cone	nose	broke	**scope**
cope	note	**choke**	**slope**
cove	poke	chose	smoke
dome	pole	close	spoke
dove	robe	**clove**	stole
hole	rode	**drone**	stone
home	rope	drove	stove
hope	rose	froze	**stroke**
hose	**tone**	globe	those
joke	**vole**	**grove**	whole
lone	vote	**probe**	wrote

u_e			
cube	**fuse**	**muse**	use
cute	mule		

Final e Phrases

cake sale	wide bike	whale tale
brave snake	whole scone	will dive in the cove
a lone mole	bike at the gate	grapes on a plate
a crate of snakes	a maze in the cave	brakes on a bike
ripe grapes	five to nine	rose on a vine
nine in line	in the shade	a fine home
will name the snake	rode to the cave	mole on his nose
pipes froze	mole hole	cute mule
drove to the game	will hide the dime	whole globe
race in the maze	five ripe plums	broke the cone
five grapes	like to drive	chose a prize
drove home	can slide home	rose in a vase
will ride a mule	can use the cube	woke the mole
ice on the lake	will take five	will laze in the glade

Final e Sentences

I will ride the white bike.	Take nine dimes back home.
Those jokes are fun to tell.	The pup broke the plate.
Let's go to the cake sale.	We plan to take the plane.
Bite the ripe green lime.	I ate the whole scone.
Tell the tale of the white whale.	The mole hole is long and wide.
The rose in the vase is pink.	We can dive in the cove.
The vole is at home in a hole.	Use the cube as a prize.
The theme of the tale is hope.	These grapes are not ripe.
Fix the bike with twine.	I wrote her a note.
The kite came in a kit.	She wore a cape on stage.
Let's ride to the cove.	Be brave and scale the hill.
There is ice on the lake.	Let's take a plane next time.
The bike is next to the gate.	A lone mole sat in a hole.
The whole globe can spin.	Hide the dime under the plate.
Kate rode the cute mule.	The fifth grade had a cake sale.
Mike can slide into home plate.	She chose a nice prize.
The tale of the brave snake is long.	The mule with the hat is so cute.
Park the bike next to the pine tree.	We rode to the cave on our bikes.

Flex Between CVC and CVCe Words

Flex between words with short vowels (CVC) and words that end in final e (CVCe) to help children distinguish between the different sounds and spellings.

CVC/CVCe Words

Short Vowel	Final e	Short Vowel	Final e
bit	bite	mad	made
can	cane	man	mane
cap	cape	mat	mate
cod	code	not	note
cub	cube	pal	pale
cut	cute	pan	pane
dim	dime	pet	Pete
fad	fade	pin	pine
fat	fate	rag	rage
fin	fine	rat	rate
hat	hate	rid	ride
hid	hide	rip	ripe
hop	hope	rob	robe
kit	kite	sit	site

Short Vowel continued	Final *e* continued	Short Vowel continued	Final *e* continued
tap	tape	quit	quite
tot	tote	scrap	scrape
us	use	shin	shine
van	vane	slid	slide
wag	wage	slim	slime
glad	glade	slop	slope
glob	globe	spin	spine
grad	grade	strip	stripe
grip	gripe	them	theme
plan	plane	twin	twine

VC/CV Words
(closed syllable/closed syllable)

A *syllable* is a unit of spoken language that contains only one vowel sound. The number of spoken vowel sounds in the word indicates the number of syllables; for example, *pet* has one syllable, and *cactus* has two syllables. A *closed syllable* has one vowel followed by one or more consonants that "close in" the vowel. The vowel sound is often short, as in *it, can, stop, bath,* or *spend.* After children learn closed syllables, they can transition to words with two closed syllables.

Teach children how to divide a longer word into smaller syllables so they can sound them out and blend them back together. Have them place dots under the vowels in the word. Then have them look between the vowels. If there are two consonants between the two vowels, have them divide the word between the consonants. In the word *napkin,* for example, dot the vowels *a* and *i.* Then divide the word between the two consonants, *p* and *k*: *nap/kin* (VC/CV).

In a multisyllabic word, one syllable has more emphasis. The syllable that has less emphasis (the non-accented vowel) is sometimes called a *schwa.* It can have the short /ŭ/ sound, as in *pencil* or *wisdom,* or the short /ĭ/ sound, as in *jacket.*

VC/CV Words

Short *a* (in initial syllable)			
admit	campus	happen	plastic
album	candid	magnet	rabbit
attic	channel	mantis	tablet
basket	frantic	mascot	tandem
cactus	gallop	napkin	traffic
Short *e* (in initial syllable)			
dentist	hectic	mental	seldom
expand	helmet	metric	selfish
expect	kennel	pellet	tennis
expel	lentil	pencil	velvet
extend	lesson	pretzel	

Short *i* (in initial syllable)			
discuss	insult	picnic	signal
hiccup	invent	pigment	tidbit
hidden	kitten	quintet	tinsel
index	limpet	ribbon	wisdom
insect	mitten		

Short *o* (in initial syllable)			
bonnet	contact	gossip	possum
bottom	content	hobbit	problem
collect	contest	hostel	tonsil
common	fossil	nostril	wombat
connect	goblin		

Short *u* (in initial syllable)			
button	nugget	rubbish	summit
custom	nutmeg	subject	trumpet
funnel	public	submit	tunnel
muffin	publish	sudden	until
mussel	puppet	suffix	upset

Multisyllable Words

VC/CV Phrases

albums in the attic	tennis lesson	public contest
kittens with mittens	collect fossils	button on tablet
muffins in a basket	plastic cactus	napkins for the picnic
upset wombat	discuss problem	trumpet lesson
velvet puppet	hidden rabbit	chicken nugget
sudden hiccup	muffin or pretzel	a common insect

VC/CV Sentences

I like chicken nuggets for lunch.	The velvet puppet lost a button.
Did you see the kittens with mittens?	The plastic cactus has sharp spines.
Do you know where the rabbit is hidden?	There was a box of albums in the attic.
Our tennis lesson will happen at ten.	Please bring napkins for the picnic.
Let's hike to the summit to collect fossils.	Do you want a muffin or a pretzel?
There is a public singing contest.	Can we discuss this math problem?

VC/CCV or VCC/CV Words

After dotting the vowels, if there are three consonants between two vowels, two of the consonants stay together. First, look for blends or digraphs. If there is a blend (con trast) or digraph (en chant), keep it together. If not, try dividing after the first consonant to see if that makes a recognizable word. If it doesn't, divide after the second consonant.

athlete	contrast	instruct	pumpkin
children	enchant	kingdom	sandwich
contract	hundred	ostrich	subtract

Inflectional Ending -s

We add the inflectional endings -s or -es to make nouns plural and to show verbs in the present tense when the subject is third-person singular (*he, she, it*). The endings -s and -es are the most common suffixes in English.

The ending -s has two sounds: /s/ and /z/. It is pronounced /z/ when it follows a voiced consonant, such as /b/, /d/, /g/, /l/, /m/, /n/, /r/, /v/, or /w/ (e.g., *dogs, runs*).

Inflectional Ending -s Words

-s /s/ in plural nouns			
bats	cups	nuts	rocks
bits	forks	plates	sacks
cats	hats	pots	tops
chips	lips	pups	trucks
-s /z/ in plural nouns			
bags	cans	jobs	**ribs**
beds	cows	mugs	stars
cabs	dogs	pens	tables
cars	hens	**rags**	tubs
-s /s/ in present-tense verbs			
asks	hops	makes	skips
cuts	jumps	naps	taps
dips	kicks	pats	**thinks**
fits	looks	sits	wants
-s /z/ in present-tense verbs			
begs	ends	runs	swims
calls	grabs	**sobs**	**tugs**
digs	**nags**	stands	yells

Inflectional Ending *-s* Phrases

cats and dogs	sits on beds	calls and yells
chips in cups	stars in the sky	hops and jumps
plates and forks	wants the chips	wants pups
kicks rocks	naps on beds	looks for nuts
calls cows	asks and begs	stands on rocks
locks the cars	fits in the bags	grabs the hats
backs of the cows	tables with forks and plates	pats the dogs

Inflectional Ending *-s* Sentences

The pens are in the mugs.	I see stars in the sky.
Set the cups on the tables.	Fred looks for nuts.
The farmer calls the cows.	He naps on the beds.
The puppy hops and jumps.	She put chips in cups.
Bobby wants pups for pets.	We need rags for the tables.
The tops of the trucks are dirty.	The dog begs for treats.
The rabbit hops and skips.	The dog wants the chips.
Hal grabs the hats off the table.	Set the table with cups and plates.
The cats and dogs hid under the sacks.	Pack plates and forks for the picnic.

Inflectional Ending -es

We add the inflectional endings -s or -es to make nouns plural and to show verbs in the present tense when the subject is third-person singular (he, she, it). We use the ending -es when the base word ends with -ss, -x, -sh, -ch, or -tch.

Inflectional Ending -es Words

ss + -es			
basses	flosses	**hisses**	messes
classes	**fusses**	kisses	misses
crosses	glasses	**lasses**	passes
dresses	**guesses**	**losses**	tosses

x + -es			
boxes	**flexes**	mixes	**tuxes**
faxes	foxes	**taxes**	waxes
fixes	**maxes**		

sh + -es			
ashes	**dashes**	lashes	rashes
brushes	fishes	leashes	rushes
bushes	flashes	mashes	**sashes**
cashes	**gashes**	**mushes**	washes
crashes	**hushes**	pushes	wishes

ch + -es			
arches	clutches	**leaches**	**pouches**
beaches	coaches	lunches	reaches
birches	couches	munches	riches
branches	**finches**	peaches	**slouches**
bunches	hunches	**perches**	**winches**
churches	inches	porches	**wrenches**

tch + -es			
batches	hatches	**notches**	squishes
catches	hitches	patches	stitches
ditches	itches	pitches	**switches**
etches	**latches**	**sketches**	watches
fetches	matches	**snatches**	

Inflectional Ending -es Phrases

glasses to see dresses	dashes to the bushes	patches the couches
hisses at the leaches	mashes and squishes	switches the sketches
etches the sketches	foxes in boxes	fixes with wrenches
reaches for fishes	washes the sashes	watches the foxes
flashes and crashes	lunches on peaches	reaches for the branches

Inflectional Ending -es Sentences

Have you seen foxes in boxes?	The snake hisses at the leaches.
I need my glasses to see all the dresses.	The artist switches the sketches at the show.
He reaches for the branches so he won't fall.	There were many patches on the couches.
He dashes to the bushes to hide.	Kangaroos with pouches jump on couches.
She mashes the bananas to make bread.	She wishes for more inches to reach the top.

Inflectional Ending *-ing*

We add the inflectional ending *-ing* to a verb to indicate the action is happening in the moment. For example, *I am standing; I was standing; I will be standing*.

In some cases, when *-ing* is added to a word its spelling might change. For example, the final consonant may be doubled (e.g., *stopping*) or the final *e* may be dropped (e.g., *liking*). However, we recommend beginning with base words in which the spelling does not change (e.g., *jumping, resting*).

Inflectional Ending *-ing* Words

No change to base word			
acting	helping	resting	testing
asking	jumping	ringing	thanking
bending	kicking	singing	thinking
blinking	**listing**	sinking	tossing
boxing	locking	smelling	trusting
brushing	missing	spilling	twisting
calling	munching	splashing	wanting
camping	passing	**springing**	washing
dressing	picking	stamping	watching
drinking	planting	standing	winking
fishing	pulling	starting	wishing
fixing	pushing	sticking	working
hanging	**renting**	telling	yelling
Double the final consonant			
fitting	hopping	running	swimming
flapping	mopping	shipping	**tipping**
grabbing	napping	stopping	winning

Drop the final *e*			
baking	giving	**sharing**	using
diving	hoping	**shining**	waking
driving	making	taking	waving

Inflectional Ending -*ing* Phrases

fishing and planting	starting swimming	resting and napping
acting and singing	pushing and pulling	hopping and jumping
camping and fishing	telling and yelling	helping and working
asking and telling	jumping and kicking	tossing and twisting
blinking and winking	drinking and munching	looking before passing

Inflectional Ending -*ing* Sentences

She is starting swimming today.	I was watching them playing.
The team is working together.	The lights are blinking.
She was asking him what to do.	The puppies are hopping and jumping.
We are acting and singing in the play.	They were pushing and pulling the rope.
Looking before passing is a safe way to bike.	They were yelling when the race was starting.
They are going camping and fishing.	The baby birds were flapping their wings.

Inflectional Ending -ed

We add the inflectional ending -ed to a verb to indicate the action happened in the past. The -ed ending has three sounds:

- /ed/ after a base word ending with a t or d (e.g., planted, landed)
- /d/ after a base word ending with a voiced consonant, such as /g/, /l/, /n/, /v/, or /z/ (e.g., pulled, filmed)
- /t/ after a base word ending with an unvoiced consonant, such as /k/, /p/, or /s/, or s, sh, x, -tch (e.g., fished, pitched)

In some cases, when -ed is added to a word its spelling might change. For example, the final consonant may be doubled (e.g., stopped) or the final e may be dropped (e.g., liked). However, we recommend beginning with words in which the spelling does not change (e.g., planted, wished, played).

Inflectional Ending -ed Words

-ed /ed/			
acted	frosted	listed	**shifted**
added	gifted	melted	**slanted**
banded	**granted**	**mended**	**squinted**
blasted	grunted	panted	**stranded**
busted	handed	planted	**tended**
chanted	hinted	printed	tested
dented	hosted	quilted	**tilted**
drafted	hunted	rented	trusted
drifted	landed	rested	twisted
dusted	lasted	rusted	wanted
ended	lifted	sanded	**winded**

-ed /d/			
banged	drilled	grilled	smelled
buzzed	filled	**longed**	spelled
called	**filmed**	pulled	spilled
clanged	**fizzed**	rolled	yelled

-ed /t/			
asked	dressed	mashed	smashed
backed	dumped	masked	sniffed
blinked	**fetched**	milked	splashed
boxed	fished	missed	stacked
brushed	fixed	mixed	stamped
bumped	**flushed**	passed	stuffed
camped	**guessed**	**pecked**	tacked
cashed	helped	picked	taxed
checked	inched	pinched	thanked
chomped	itched	**plucked**	trashed
clashed	jumped	pressed	tricked
cracked	kicked	pushed	**tucked**
crunched	licked	rushed	watched
crushed	locked	**shocked**	wished

Inflectional Ending -*ed* Phrases

fixed and mended	called and yelled	jumped and landed
banged and clanged	checked the tent	stacked the boxes
helped and washed	frosted the cake	stuffed and grilled
spilled the milk	melted the ice	twisted and pulled
planted and tended	filled the box	pushed and pulled
jumped and splashed	bumped and smashed	stuffed and grilled fish
dressed for the party	crunched on carrot sticks	chomped and crunched

Inflectional Ending -*ed* Sentences

She helped Dad wash the car.	The baby spilled the milk.
Ted twisted and pulled the taffy.	The dog licked the frosted cake.
Who filled the box with candy?	She yelled but no one heard her.
We rested after we mended the shed.	They checked the tent before they camped.
The pans and pots banged and clanged.	They helped us and fixed the car.
We jumped and splashed in the pond.	We watched as they acted in the play.
After we landed, we jumped off the boat.	We stacked the sticks in the yard.
Mom stuffed and grilled the fish.	Bob planted seeds and tended the garden.

Suffixes -*er*, -*est*

We use the suffix -*er* to indicate a person who does something, as in *teacher*. We also use the suffix -*er* to compare two things, as in *colder*. The suffix -*est* compares three or more things.

In some cases, when -*er* or -*est* is added to a word its spelling might change. For example, the final consonant may be doubled (e.g., *bigger*) or the final e may be dropped (e.g., *maker*). However, we recommend beginning with words in which the spelling does not change (e.g., *taller, tallest*).

Suffix -*er* Words (person who does something)

No change to base word			
banker	farmer	planter	swinger
blocker	fisher	seller	teacher
boxer	jumper	singer	tester
caller	packer	splasher	washer
catcher	painter		
Double the final consonant			
drummer	runner	swimmer	winner
jogger			
Drop the final e			
baker	driver	racer	voter
biker	maker	rider	writer
diver			

Suffix *-er, -est* Words (comparing two or more things)

No change to base word			
colder	coldest	quicker	quickest
darker	darkest	shorter	shortest
faster	fastest	slower	slowest
fewer	fewest	smaller	smallest
fuller	fullest	softer	softest
harder	hardest	taller	tallest
longer	longest	thicker	thickest
older	oldest	warmer	warmest
Double the final consonant			
bigger	biggest	sadder	saddest
gladder	gladdest	thinner	thinnest
hotter	hottest	wetter	wettest
madder	maddest		
Drop the final *e*			
finer	finest	wider	widest
nicer	nicest	wiser	wisest
safer	safest		

Suffix -er, -est Phrases

quickest drummer	fastest runner	smaller but quicker
teacher and writer	longest sock	drummer and singer
safest driver	nicest baker	strongest swimmer
widest part	slowest racer	plant fewer seeds
older and wiser	thickest and softest	washer was wetter

Suffix -er, -est Sentences

He is a drummer and singer.	Sandra knit the longest sock.
Gus is the safest driver.	The slowest racer came last.
The teacher and writer wrote a book together.	He is the quickest drummer I have ever seen.
The widest part of the river is near my home.	The farmer planted fewer seeds today.
It's hotter where the baker works.	We crossed the river at the widest part.
She is the strongest swimmer on the team.	She chose the thickest and softest blanket.
This sock is longer than the other one.	The winner will be the fastest runner.
The rabbit is smaller but quicker than the dog.	She is older and wiser than I am.

Irregular High-Frequency Words

A high-frequency word may be decodable (can be sounded out), temporarily irregular (challenging for the child to decode at that moment because the spelling patterns found in that word have not yet been introduced), or irregular (not spelled the way it sounds). Help children understand that most words are phonetically predictable and regular, and over time as they become more proficient at reading, many of the temporarily irregular words will no longer be irregular.

This list contains high-frequency words that are irregular for kindergarten and first grade. Children need to memorize the sequence of letters in each word for reading and spelling, although some of the letters may provide clues. For example, in the word *said*, the initial and final sounds (/s/ and /d/) are reliable, while the medial letters *ai* have a variable vowel sound. Show children what parts of the word are regular and what parts are irregular. Model high-frequency words in sentences to show how they are used. Then encourage children to generate their own meaningful sentences.

To practice, write the words on a sheet of paper and have children trace each word, copy it, and then cover the word and write it from memory. You can also use a folding sentence strip for children to write, trace, and copy words. Then they fold over the sentence strip to cover the words they have already written and rewrite each word from memory without looking at the practice words. Unfold to check.

Irregular High-Frequency Words

a	done	once	they
again	eight	one	through
are	four	other	to
been	from	people	today
both	give	pretty	together
buy	have	put	two
carry	I	said	very
come	laugh	shall	want
could	live	some	warm
do	many	the	was
does	most	their	wash
don't	of	there	water

Irregular High-Frequency Words continued			
were	who	work	you
what	word	would	your
where	words		

Phrases and Sentences for
Select Irregular High-Frequency Words

Words	Phrases	Sentences
a	a cat	A cat is the best pet!
from	from Dad	I got a gift from Dad.
of	of milk	A glass of milk is good to drink.
one	one cat	She has one cat.
put	put it	Put it on the table.
said	said "hi"	She said "hi."
the	the fox	The fox is red and fast.
to	to the store	We went to the store.
two	two dogs	Two dogs are better than one.
there	here to there	We walked from here to there.
they	they can	They can come to the farm.
was	was hot	It was hot out.
what	what did	What did you bring?
where	where is	Where is the bug?
you	you and I	You and I will sit here.

Compound Words

Compound words are two individual words joined together to create a new word. They are an excellent way to teach children how to read longer words. Compound words are divided between the two smaller words. For some compound words, children can illustrate the two little words and discuss the related meaning: *basket + ball = basketball*; *hay + stack = haystack*; *blue + berry = blueberry*.

Compound Words

A			
afternoon	anteater	anything	armchair
airplane	anthill	anytime	armrest
airtight	anybody	applesauce	
B			
backbone	baseball	birdbath	bookmark
backdoor	basketball	birdcage	breakfast
backpack	bathrobe	birdcall	broomstick
backstage	bathroom	birthday	bulldog
backstroke	bathtub	blackbird	bullfrog
backyard	bedroom	blueberry	butterfly
bagpipe	bedside	bluebird	buttermilk
barnyard	bedtime	bookcase	
C			
campfire	cheerleader	cookbook	cowboy
campground	classroom	cornbread	crossword
candlelight	clothespin	cornfield	cupcake
cardboard	clubhouse	countdown	

D			
daydream	doorbell	downstairs	driveway
daylight	doorknob	downtown	drumstick
doghouse	doormat	dragonfly	dugout
dollhouse	downhill		

E			
eardrum	everybody	everywhere	eyeglasses
earthquake	everyday	eyeball	eyelid
eggshell	everything		

F			
faraway	firefighter	fireworks	footrest
farmhouse	firefly	flowerpot	footstep
fingernail	firehouse	football	footstool
fingertip	fireplace	footprint	

G			
goldfish	grasshopper	greenhouse	grown-up

H			
hairbrush	handprint	headphone	hometown
haircut	handshake	headstand	homework
hairpin	handstand	hilltop	honeybee
hairstyle	handwrite	homemade	horseback
handbag	headache	homeroom	horseshoe
handball	headband	homesick	hotdog
handpick			

I, J, K			
inside	jellyfish	keyboard	

L			
lapdog	lighthouse	lookout	lunchroom
lifetime			

M			
mailbox	moonlight	motorcycle	mousetrap
milkshake	motorboat		

N			
newspaper	nightgown	notebook	

O			
outdoors	outfield	outside	overnight

P			
pancake	pinecone	playpen	popcorn
peanut	playground	pocketbook	postcard
pillowcase	playhouse		

R			
railroad	raindrop	roadside	rosebud
rainbow	rainfall	rooftop	rowboat
raincoat			

S			
sailboat	scarecrow	seafood	seashore
sandbox	scrapbook	seaport	seaside
sandpaper	seagull	seashell	seatbelt

S continued			
seaweed	snowman	something	sunburn
sidewalk	snowplow	spaceship	sunflower
sideways	snowshoe	spacesuit	sunlight
skyline	snowstorm	springtime	sunrise
snapshot	snowsuit	starfish	sunset
snowball	somebody	starlight	sunshine
snowfall	someday	steamboat	supermarket
snowflake	someone	storyteller	

T			
tablespoon	tightrope	toothache	treehouse
teacup	toenail	toothbrush	treetop
teaspoon	toolbox	toothpaste	tugboat
thunderstorm			

U			
underground	underwater	uphill	upstairs

W			
wallpaper	wheelchair	windshield	workday
washcloth	whiteboard	wintertime	worktable
watchdog	windmill	wishbone	wristwatch
waterfall	windpipe	workbench	

Compound Words Phrases

seafood cookbook	uphill on horseback	bedroom upstairs
blueberry pancakes	bullfrog underwater	airplane in the afternoon
notebook in my backpack	newspaper in the mailbox	starfish on the seashore
plays basketball and football	washcloth by the bathtub	honeybee on the sunflower
seashore by moonlight	milkshake and a cupcake	homemade cornbread
whiteboard in the classroom	snowflake on sidewalk	rainbow after a thunderstorm

Compound Words Sentences

We flew on the airplane in the afternoon.	We saw the starfish on the seashore.
I always keep a notebook in my backpack.	The snowflakes melted on the sidewalk.
I love blueberry pancakes for breakfast.	I want to have cupcakes for my birthday.
The newspaper is in the mailbox.	A raincoat helps you stay dry from the raindrops.
There was a lovely rainbow after the thunderstorm.	We rode uphill on horseback.
Did you see the honeybee on the sunflower?	We ate homemade cornbread for breakfast.

Follow the Path

Players move along a game path as they search for words that contain target phonics skills.

Number of Players: 2 to 4

You'll Need: Follow the Path game board (pages 114–115) • Vowel Cards (page 116) • Star Cards (page 117) • scissors • tape • file folder (optional) • game pieces (e.g., buttons)

Setting Up the Game

Make a copy of the blank Follow the Path game board. Decide what phonics pattern or skill you want children to practice (for example, VCe or final-e words). Find the corresponding word lists in the book and choose words for the game. Write the words in the blank spaces on the game board. To assemble the game board, fold along the dotted line (B) and tape (B) to (A) as indicated. (**Option:** Glue or tape the game board to the inside of a file folder to make it sturdier.)

Make two copies of the Vowel Cards page on cardstock and cut the cards apart, including the cards with a large star on them. Shuffle the cards and stack them face down on the Vowel Cards space on the game board. (**Note:** You can use the Vowel Cards with most single-syllable words in this book: CVC, blends, digraphs, Floss, and VCe.)

Photocopy the Star Cards page on cardstock and cut the cards apart. Shuffle the cards and stack them face down on the Star Cards space on the game board. Provide each player with a game piece.

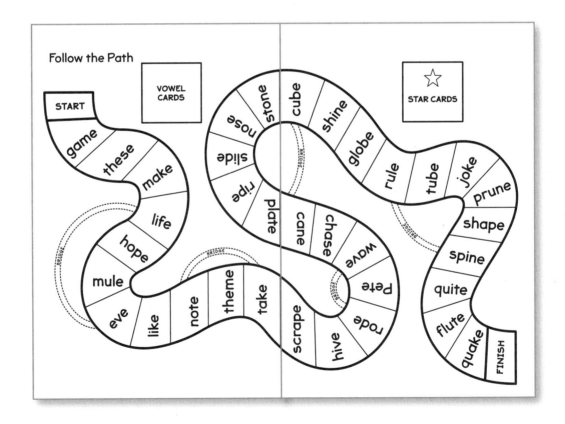

How to Play

1. Players place their game pieces on START. Then they take turns picking a card from the top of the Vowel Cards pile.
   - If players get a Vowel Card, they move their game piece to the first word that has that vowel and read the word.
   - If players get a card with a star on it, they take a card from the top of the Star Card pile and follow the directions.
2. If players land on a space with a bridge, they can "cross" the bridge and advance to the connected space. They must read both words.
3. Players continue taking turns until a player reaches FINISH.
4. The first player to reach FINISH wins the game.

Going Further

- For additional practice, make extra copies of the game board for children to take home and play with their families.
- Customize the game by creating your own game cards to target other phonics skills. r

Follow the Path

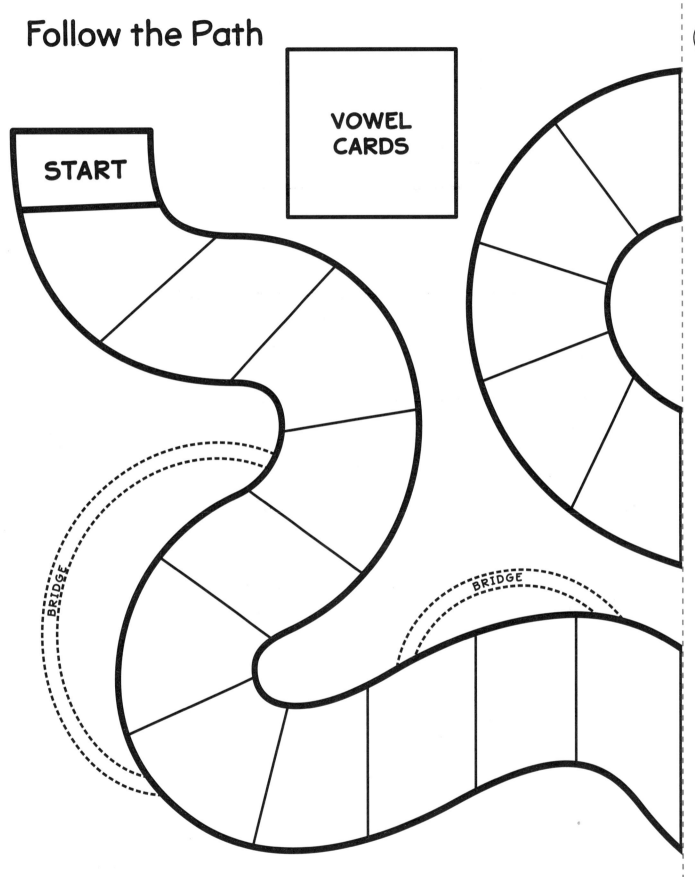

VOWEL CARDS

START

BRIDGE

BRIDGE

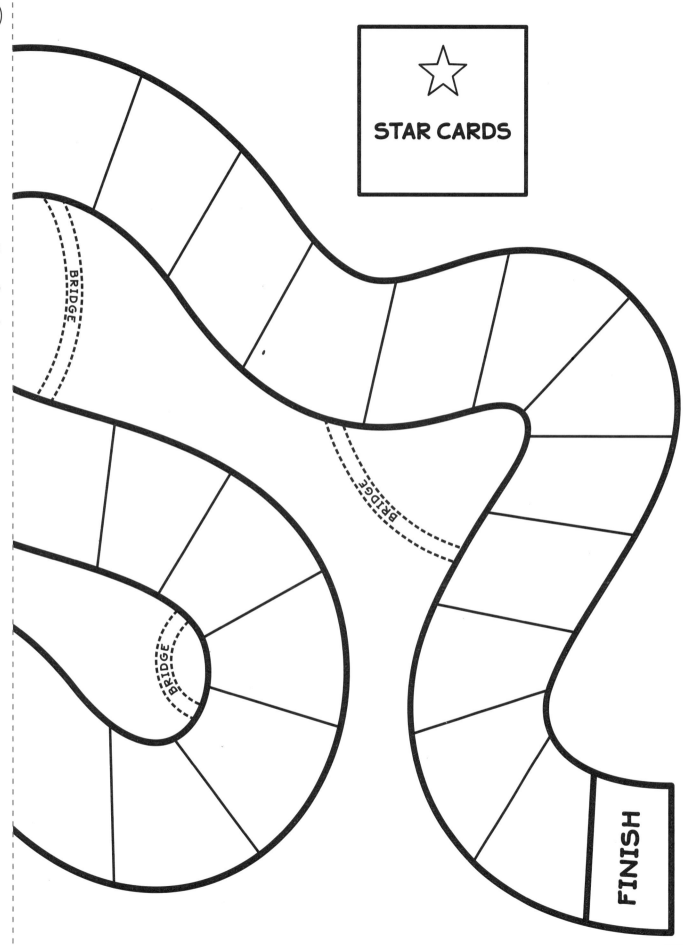

STAR CARDS

BRIDGE

BRIDGE

BRIDGE

FINISH

Fold or cut on dotted line. Attach to page **A**.

Follow the Path: Vowel Cards

a	a	a	☆
e	e	e	☆
i	i	i	☆
o	o	o	☆
u	u	u	☆

Follow the Path: Star Cards

☆ Move ahead 2 spaces.	☆ Say a word that rhymes with the word you are on.	☆ Read the last 5 words.	☆ Move to the nearest bridge and cross it.
☆ Move back 2 spaces.	☆ Take an extra turn.	☆ Read all the words from START to your game piece.	☆ Say a word that begins with the same sound as the word you are on.
☆ Read the last 5 words.	☆ Move to the nearest bridge and cross it.	☆ Skip a turn.	☆ Say a word that rhymes with the word you are on.
☆ Read all the words from START to your game piece.	☆ Take an extra turn.	☆ Move back 2 spaces.	☆ Move ahead 2 spaces.
☆ Skip a turn.	☆ Choose a word from the game board. Use it in a sentence.	☆ Say a word that begins with the same sound as the word you are on.	☆ Choose a word from the game board. Use it in a sentence.

Roll and Read

Children build fluency as they read columns of words in this simple game.

Number of Players: 2

You'll Need: Roll and Read activity sheet (page 119) • number cube • crayons or colored pencils

Setting Up the Activity

Make a copy of the blank Roll and Read activity sheet. Decide what phonics pattern or skill you want children to practice (for example, digraphs). Find the corresponding word lists in the book and choose words for the activity. Write the words in the blank spaces on the activity sheet. Then make a copy for each player.

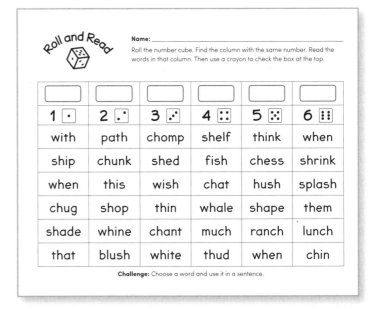

Provide players with a colored pencil or crayon of their choice to use throughout the game.

✂

How to Play

1. Players take turns rolling a number cube to see which column of words to read.

2. At their turn, players read all the words in that column. (Have an adult check for accuracy.)

3. After players finish reading the list, they place a checkmark in the box at the top of the column. (**Note:** Players can read a column more than once.)

4. Players continue taking turns until each column has two checks or until a specified time limit has been met. (Players can set the number of checks per game.)

Going Further

- Challenge players to pick a word from a column and use it in a sentence.
- Allow players to read the list from top to bottom or from bottom to top.
- For additional practice, make extra copies of the activity sheet for children to take home and play with their families.

Roll and Read

Name: _____

Roll the number cube. Find the column with the same number. Read the words in that column. Then use a crayon to check the box at the top.

☐	☐	☐	☐	☐	☐
1 •	2 •	3 ••	4 ••	5 ••	6 •••

Challenge: Choose a word and use it in a sentence.

Fluency Voices

Add drama and excitement to fluency practice with this activity that challenges children to read a list of words using different voices.

Number of Players: 2

You'll Need: Fluency Voices activity sheet (page 121) • 2 paper clips • number cube

Setting Up the Activity

Make a copy of the blank Fluency Voices activity sheet. Decide what phonics pattern or skill you want children to practice (for example, multisyllable words VC/CV). Find the corresponding word lists in the book and choose words for the game. Write the words in the blank spaces on the sheet. Then make as many copies of the activity sheet as needed.

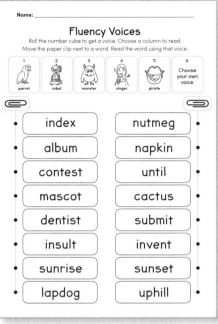

Place one paper clip along the left edge of the activity sheet and another paper clip along its right edge. Players slide the paper clip up or down the list to highlight the word they are reading.

How to Play

1. Players take turns rolling a number cube to get a character on the top of the page.

2. At their turn, players choose a column, move the paper clip to a word, and read the word using the character's voice.

3. Players continue taking turns until each child has read at least five words (or until a specified time limit has been met).

Going Further

- Create and photocopy multiple lists to make booklets for children to practice various phonics skills with multiple character voices.

- For additional practice, make extra copies of the activity sheet for children to take home and play with their families.

Name: _____

Fluency Voices

Roll the number cube to get a voice. Choose a column to read.
Move the paper clip next to a word. Read the word using that voice.

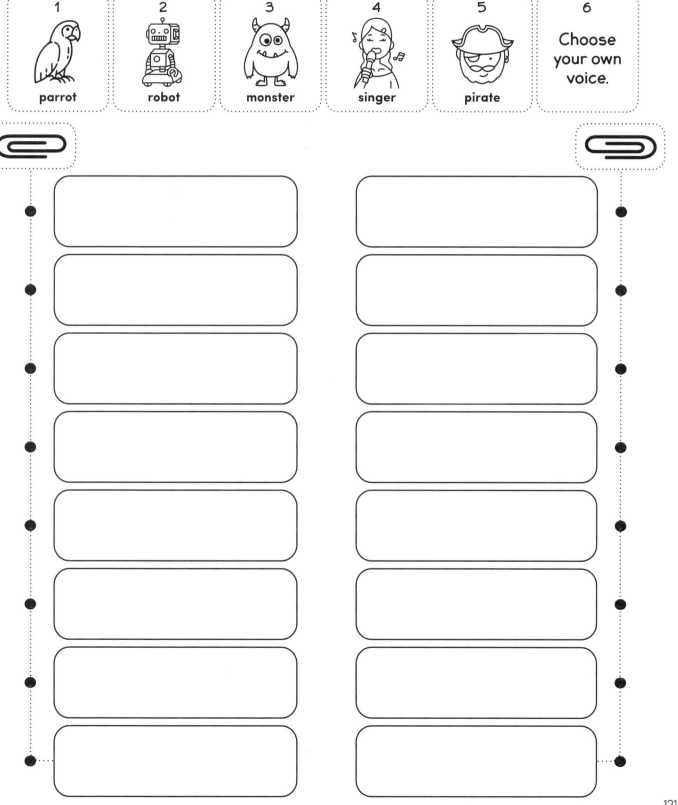

Sort It Out!

This word-sort activity is perfect for two children to work on collaboratively or for independent practice.

Number of Players: 1 or 2

You'll Need: Sort It Out! chart (page 123) • Sort It Out! Blank Word Cards (page 124)

Setting Up the Activity

Make a copy of the blank Sort It Out! chart and the Blank Word Cards sheet. Choose two contrasting phonics or spelling patterns for children to sort (for example, -ch and -tch). At the top of the chart in the dotted boxes, write the two phonics patterns as headers.

Next, find the corresponding word lists in the book. Decide how many words you want children to sort. On the blank word cards, write words from the lists that highlight the two patterns. (**Note:** Consider creating a self-checking answer key, so children can check their sorts. Make an extra copy of the Sort It Out! Blank Word Cards and fill it in with the correct answers.) Shuffle the word cards and stack them face down next to the Sort It Out! chart.

| Name: _____ |
| Sort It Out! |

-ch	-tch
ranch	switch
lunch	fetch
pinch	pitch
hunch	catch
branch	itch
inch	hatch
finch	scratch
clench	sketch

How to Play

1. Players take turns picking a word card, reading the word, and deciding where the card belongs on the Sort It Out! chart.

2. The other player may either agree or disagree with where the card was placed. If players don't agree, they can refer to an adult or the self-checking answer key.

3. After all the cards have been sorted, players can check their chart with the answer key.

Going Further

- Encourage children to verbalize why they placed the words in the respective columns.

- For extra challenge, leave off part of the words (for example, *bea__* and *ba__*). Sorting -ch and -tch words, for example, becomes more meaningful when children need to decide which ending is correct. It helps reinforce that the longer spelling is used after a short vowel.

- For additional practice, make extra copies of the chart and word cards for children to take home and play with their families.

Sort It Out!

Sort It Out! Blank Word Cards

Fishing for Words

In this two-player game, children "fish" for word cards and collect as many words as possible.

Number of Players: 2

You'll Need: Fishing for Words game board (page 127) • Fish Word Cards (pages 128–129) • crayons or colored pencils

Setting Up the Game

Make a copy of the Fishing for Words game board and the blank Fish Word Cards. Decide what phonics pattern or skill you want children to practice (for example, inflectional ending -ed). Find the corresponding word lists in the book and choose words for the game. Then write one or two words in each blank Fish Word Card.

Cut out the number cards (1, 2, 3) and the Fish Word Cards. Create three piles of Fish Word Cards according to the number on each card. Gather all the "1" cards and stack them face down under number card "1." Do the same for the "2" cards and the "3" cards.

Place the game board near the stacks of Fish Word Cards, within easy reach of both players. Provide each player with a different-colored crayon or pencil.

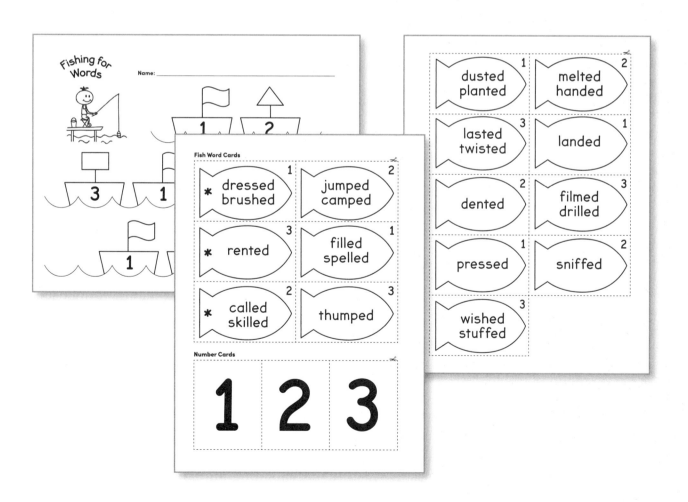

How to Play

1. Players take turns choosing a boat on the game board to color in.

2. At their turn, players take a Fish Word Card from the number pile that matches the number on the boat they chose. (That boat will no longer be available to the other player.) For example, if a player chooses a boat with "2" on it, they color the boat and pick a Fish Word Card from pile 2.

   - The player reads the word(s) on the Fish Word Card and keeps the card.
   - If the player gets a Fish Word Card with a ✱ on it, they have picked a bonus card. The player then reads the word(s) on the card, keeps it, and picks another card from the same pile to read.

3. Players continue taking turns until all the Fish Word Cards are gone.

4. Players count the number of words on all their cards. The player with the higher number of words (not cards) wins.

Going Further

- For added fun, attach paper clips to the Fish Word Cards. Use a pencil, a piece of string, and a small magnet to create a fishing pole for each player. Children can "fish" for their Fish Word Cards.

- Make additional copies of the Fish Word Cards for extended play.

- For additional practice, make extra copies of the game board and cards for children to take home and play with their families.

Fishing for Words

Name: _____

3

1 1

2 2

3 3

1 1

2 2

3 3

127

Fish Word Cards

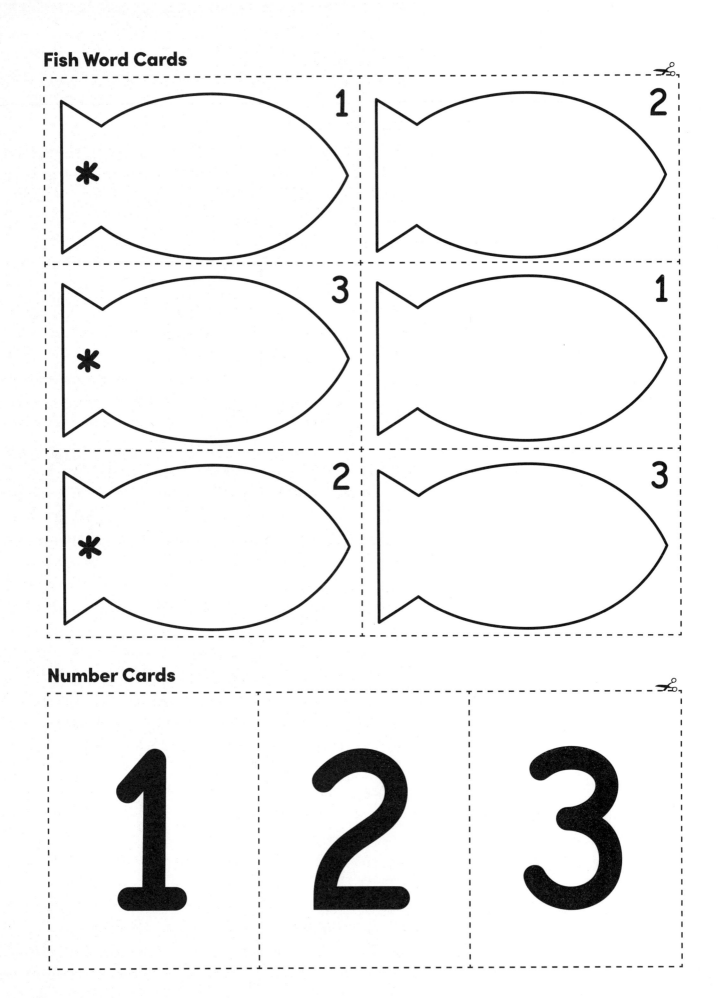

Number Cards

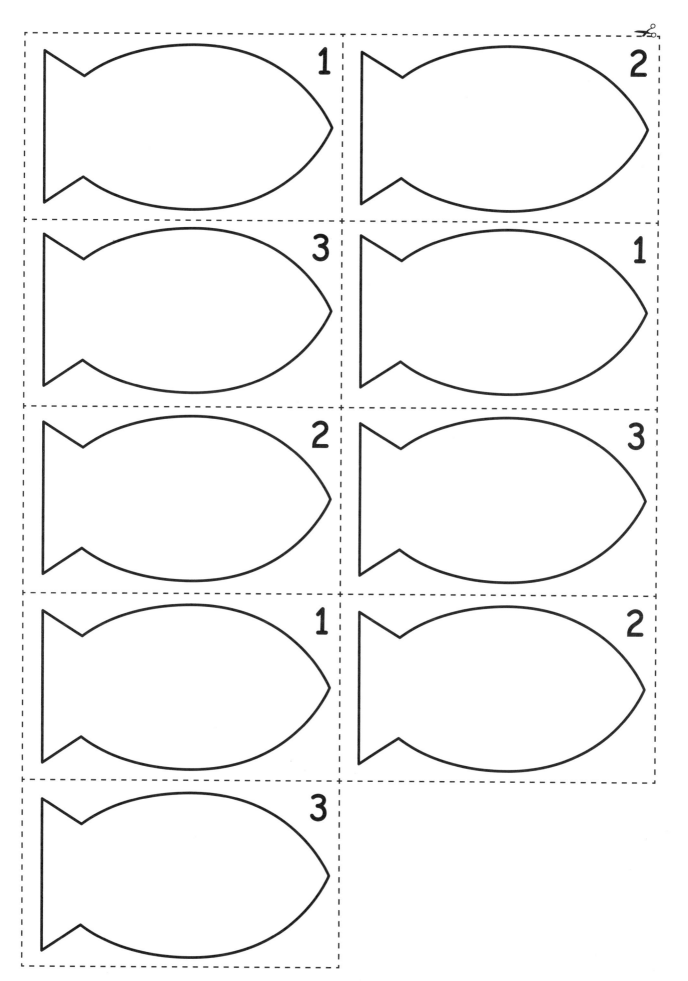

Bunches of Balloons

Watch children's confidence soar as they practice reading words while coloring balloons.

Number of Players: 2

You'll Need: Bunches of Balloons game board (page 132) • Bunches of Balloons Spinner (page 133) • pencil and paper clip (for the spinner) • different color pencils

Setting Up the Game

Make a copy of the blank Bunches of Balloons game board and the spinner. Decide what phonics pattern or skill you want children to practice (for example, consonant blends). Find the corresponding word lists in the book and choose words for the game. Write one or two words in each blank balloon on the game board.

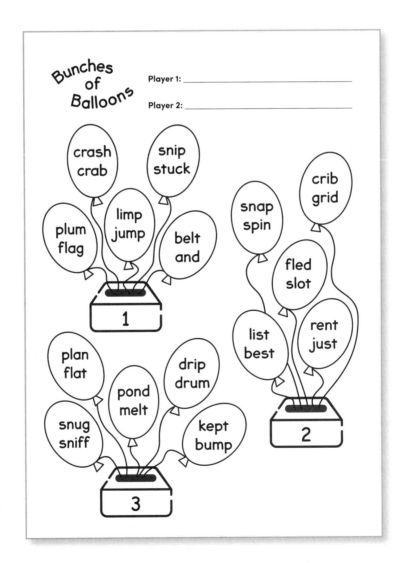

For the spinner, provide players with a pencil and paper clip to use as a spinner. Show them how to use the spinner: Hold the pencil upright on the circle in the middle of the spinner. Place the paper clip at the bottom of the pencil. With your fingers, flick the paper clip to use it as a spinner.

Provide players with a colored pencil of their choice to use throughout the game.

Note: Under the spinner is a "Workspace." If a child is struggling to read a word, use the space provided to model strategies to help the child decode the word.

How to Play

1. Using their colored pencil, players write their names on the top of the page.
2. Players take turns spinning the spinner.
   - If players spin a number (1, 2, or 3), they choose a balloon from the basket with the corresponding number and read the words on that balloon. If players read the words correctly, they can color that balloon.
   - If players spin "Free Choice," they may choose a balloon from any basket, read the words, and color in the balloon.
3. Players continue taking turns until all the balloons are colored.
4. A player can claim a basket (or bunch) of balloons if he or she has colored in more balloons in that basket than the other player. The player who claims the most bunches of balloons wins.

Going Further

- For additional practice, make extra copies of the game board and spinner for children to take home and play with their families.

Bunches of Balloons

Player 1: _____

Player 2: _____

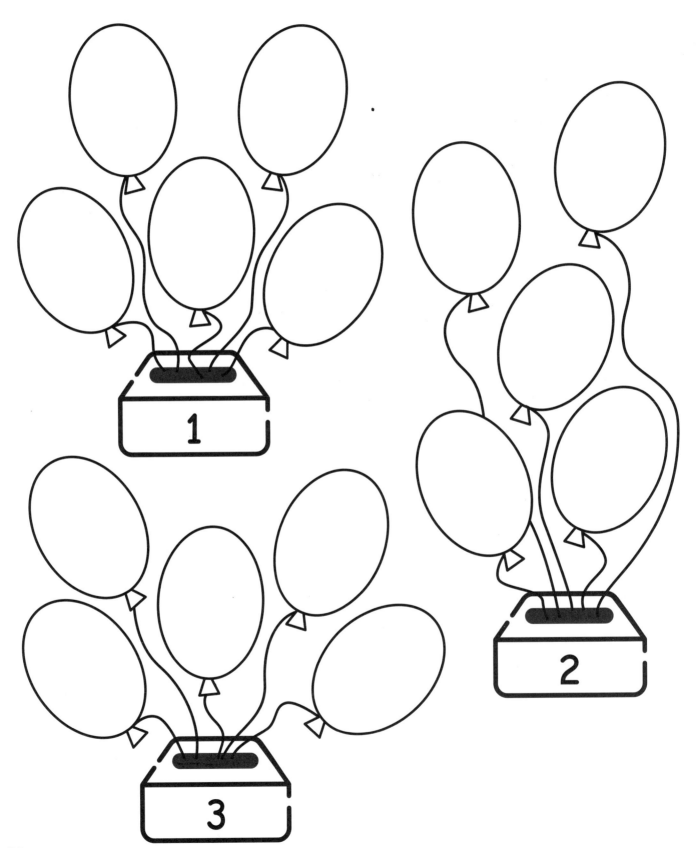

Bunches of Balloons Spinner

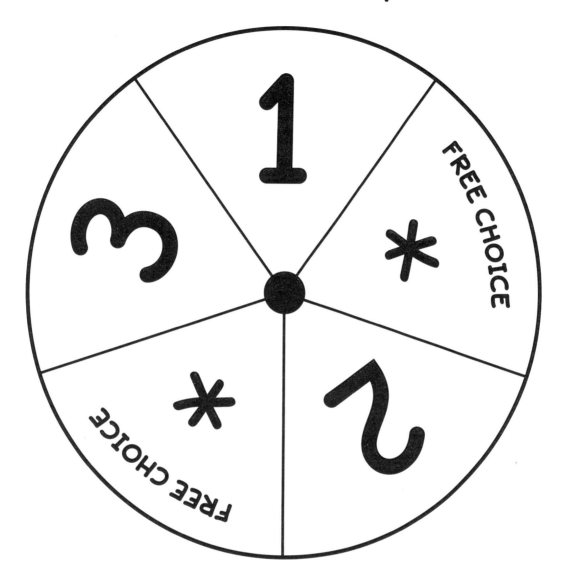

Workspace

Sentence Scramble

Children build language arts skills as they reconstruct scrambled sentences.

You'll Need: Sentence Scramble activity sheet (page 135) • scissors • glue or tape • pencils

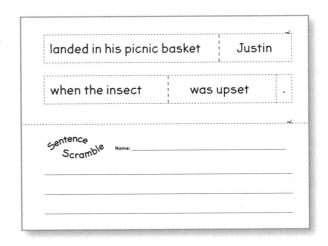

Setting Up the Activity

Make copies of the blank Sentence Scramble activity sheet to fill in. (Note: Each sheet is designed for only one sentence.) Decide what phonics pattern or skill you want children to practice (for example, multisyllabic words). Find the corresponding sentence list in the book and choose one or more sentences. You might also create your own sentences using the corresponding word lists. Consider including words from recently taught skills as well.

Scramble each sentence, clustering the words into meaningful chunks. (For example: *chicken nuggets | I like | for lunch*.) Write the scrambled chunks for each sentence on the two blank strips at the top of the activity sheet. Draw a dotted vertical line between the chunks to separate them. Make a copy of the filled-in Sentence Scramble activity sheet for each child.

How to Play

1. Cut the horizontal dotted line to separate the top part and bottom part of the Sentence Scramble activity sheet. Set aside the bottom part.

2. Cut apart the Sentence Scramble strips along the dotted lines. Read the chunks.

3. On your desk or table, move around the pieces to make a meaningful sentence. Some sentences may be arranged in more than one way.

4. Glue or tape the unscrambled pieces to the bottom part of the page. Or write the complete sentence on the lines.

Going Further

- Make multiple copies of various scrambled sentence worksheets and create a Sentence Scramble box for additional independent practice in class.

- If children are ready, use scrambled sentences as a springboard to teach beginning sentence structure; beginning grammar concepts, such as nouns and verbs; and punctuation.

- Consider changing the period into a question mark and write a question.

- Invite children to illustrate their sentences.

- For additional practice, make extra copies of the activity sheet for children to take home.

Sentence Scramble

Name: _____

135

The Elevator Game

Players "ride" up and down the elevator as they identify words with specific phonics patterns.

Number of Players: 2

You'll Need: Elevator Game Board (page 137) • Elevator Game Cards (page 138) • game pieces (e.g., buttons, coins) • crayons

Setting Up the Game

Make a copy of the blank Elevator Game Board. Choose two phonics patterns or skills you want children to practice (for example, -ng and-nk; short i and short e; closed syllable and vowel-consonant-e syllable). Find the corresponding word lists in the book and choose words for the game. You will need an equal number of words for each pattern/skill. Choose comparable words from both patterns/skills, so the game is fair for both players. On the game board, write a word on each blank "floor" of the building.

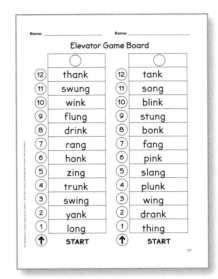

Next, write the phonics pattern/skills on the Elevator Game Cards. For example, if you wrote -ng and -nk words on the "floors," then write -ng or -nk on the game cards. Make sure there is an equal number of cards for each skill. Cut apart the game cards. Include the eight numbered arrow cards that send players up or down floors. Provide each player with a game piece.

How to Play

1. Shuffle the Elevator Game Cards and arrow cards. Stack them face down near the game board. Both players place their game pieces at the bottom floor (Start).

2. Players take turns picking a game card from the stack.

    *   If players get a card with a phonic element on it, they move up to the first word that contains that element. For example, if players pick an -ng card, they move up to the first -ng word in their elevator and read the word aloud.

    *   If players get an ↑ or ↓ card, they move their playing piece up or down the number of floors on the card. They then read the word on the space where they land.

3. Players continue taking turns until one player reaches the top floor. That player colors in the circle on the top of the column. (**Option:** Have the player read all the words in the elevator correctly to win.)

Going Further

*   For young children, 12 words might be too many. Instead, write words on every other floor and tell children the elevator stops only at odd (or even) floors.

*   For additional practice, make extra copies of the game board for children to take home and play with their families.

Name: _____   Name: _____

Elevator Game Board

12	( )
11	
10	
9	
8	
7	
6	
5	
4	
3	
2	
1	

↑ **START**

12	( )
11	
10	
9	
8	
7	
6	
5	
4	
3	
2	
1	

↑ **START**

Elevator Game Cards

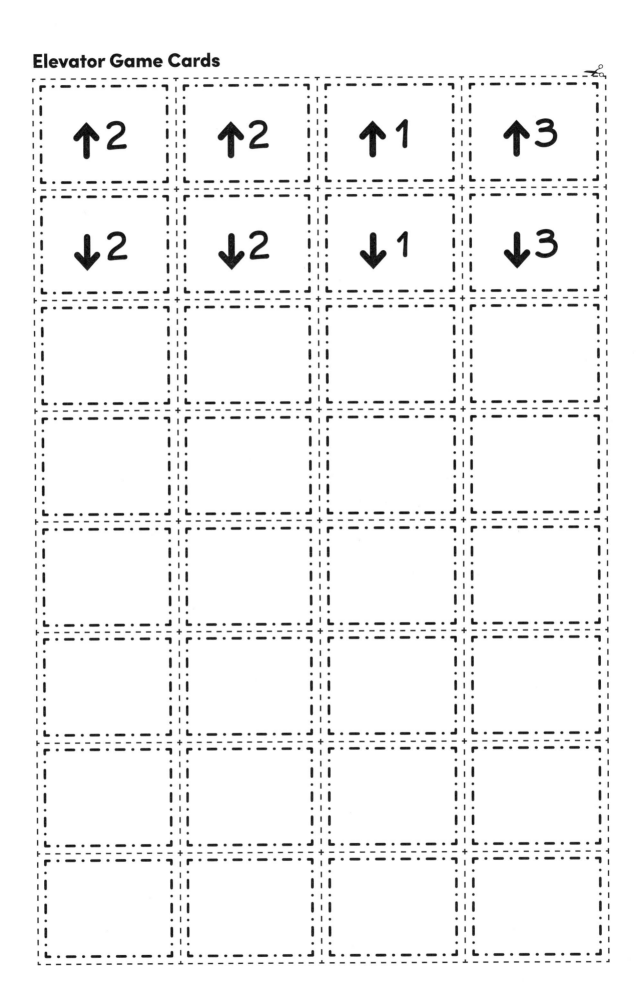

Animals In!

Collecting and reading word cards may seem easy but watch out for the animals! They just might steal all the cards away.

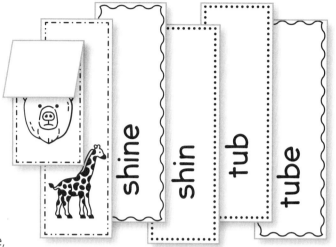

Number of Players: 2 or more

You'll Need: Animals In! Cards (pages 140–141)
• deep container (e.g., large paper bag, basket)

Setting Up the Game

Make as many copies as you need of the blank Animals In! Cards. Decide what phonics pattern or skill you want children to practice (for example, vowel-consonant-e). Find the corresponding word lists in the book and choose words for the game. Then write one word on each blank card. Do not write on the animal cards. Cut apart the cards (including the four animal cards) and fold them in half so children cannot see the words or pictures. Place all the folded cards in a deep container.

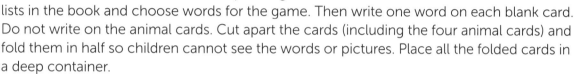

How to Play

1. Players take turns picking a folded card from the container. At their turn, players read the word on the card and then keep it.

2. If players get an animal card, they must return all the word cards they have collected back to the container. Don't return the animal card to the container. Once an animal card has been picked, it is discarded for that game.
(**Option:** If players pick an animal card, they can take two cards from each of their opponents. Once an animal card has been picked, it is discarded for that game.)

3. Players continue taking turns until the container is empty. The player who collects the most word cards wins.

Going Further

• Have children sort the words when they finish the game. Invite them to reread the words for fluency practice.

• Consider adding nonsense words to the back of each strip for more practice with the phonics pattern.

• For additional practice, make extra copies of the Animals In! Cards and word cards for children to take home and play with their families.

Animals In! Cards

Animals In! Cards

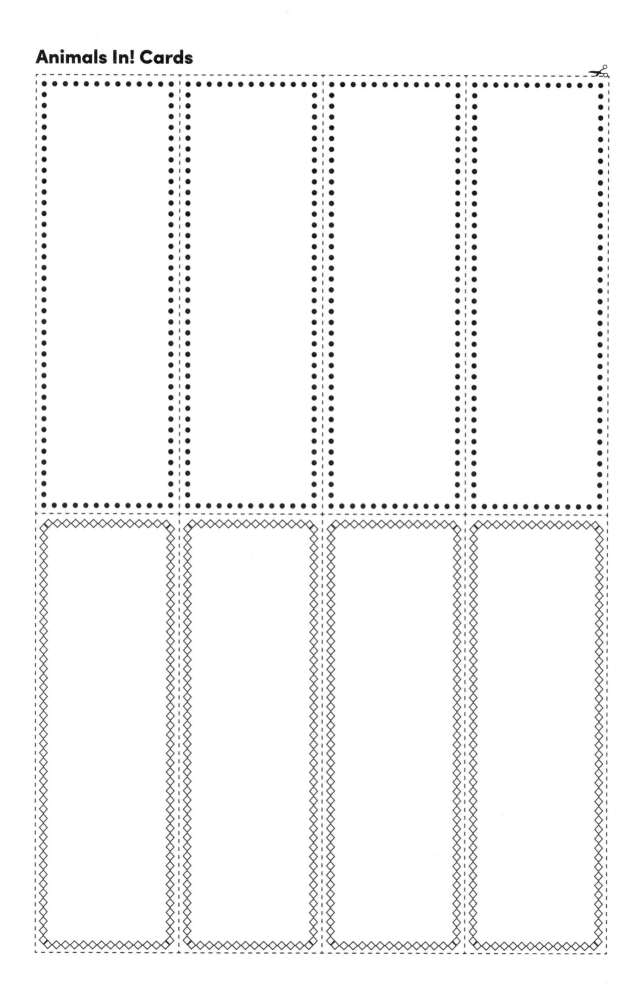

Word! Wham! Wow!

Build children's spelling skills with this small-group activity that has children filling in their own game board before playing.

Number of Players: 2 or more

You'll Need: Word! Wham! Wow! game board (page 143) • Master Word List (page 144) • pencils • dry-erase board or chart paper

Setting Up the Game

Make a copy of the blank Word! Wham! Wow! game board for each child. Decide what phonics pattern or skill you want children to practice (for example, inflectional ending -ing). Find the corresponding word lists in the book and choose nine words for the game. Write the words in the Master Word List. Then, provide children with pencils to fill in their own game boards.

Name: _____

Word! Wham! Wow! Game Board

	boxing	twisting
bending banding		splashing
brushing	sniffing snifing	

143

How to Play

1. Provide each child with a blank Word! Wham! Wow! game board.

2. Dictate a word from the Master Word List.

3. Players choose one of the blank spaces on their game board and spell the dictated word in the space.

4. Spell the word aloud and write it on a dry-erase board or chart paper for children to see. Have children check their own spelling. **Note:** It is very important to quickly check each child's spelling. Make sure all children in the group have every word spelled correctly before the game begins. If players misspell a word, have them cross it out and correct it.

5. After players have correctly spelled all nine words on their game board, the game begins.

6. To play, a teacher calls out one of the nine words from the Master Word List. Players then cross out the word on their own game board. Play continues with the teacher calling out another word for players to cross off.

7. If a player crosses off three words in a row, he or she should call out, "Word! Wham! Wow!" The player then reads and spells the three words correctly. The first player to do so wins the game.

Going Further

- Have more advanced students name a rhyming word or a synonym or antonym of the word.
- For additional practice, make extra copies of the game board and word lists for children to take home and play with their families.

Word! Wham! Wow!

Name: _____

Word! Wham! Wow!
(Master Word List)

SKILL FOCUS:

1. _____

2. _____

3. _____

4. _____

5. _____

6. _____

7. _____

8. _____

9. _____

Notes: _____

_____

_____